# ALL THE LOVE WE NEED

---

*ROD THOMAS*

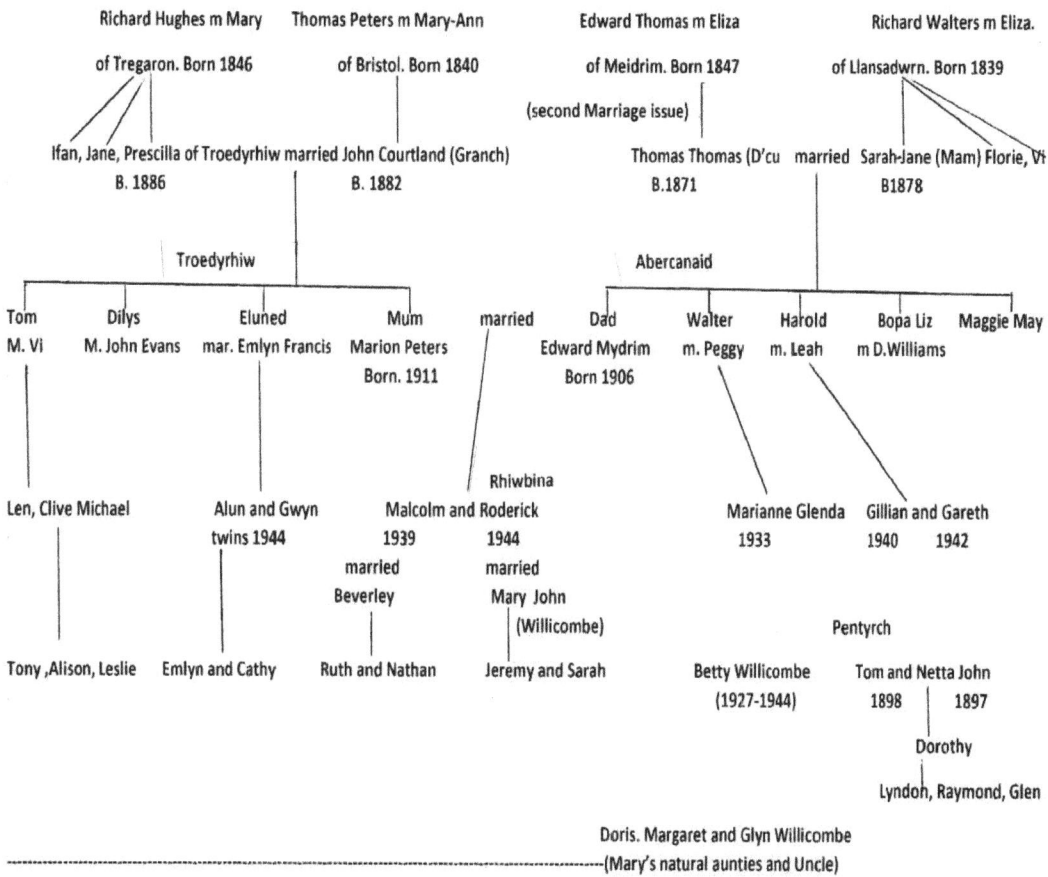

Richard Hughes m Mary     Thomas Peters m Mary-Ann     Edward Thomas m Eliza     Richard Walters m Eliza.

of Tregaron. Born 1846     of Bristol. Born 1840     of Meidrim. Born 1847     of Llansadwrn. Born 1839

(second Marriage issue)

Ifan, Jane, Prescilla of Troedyrhiw married John Courtland (Granch)     Thomas Thomas (D'cu)   married   Sarah-Jane (Mam) Florie, Vi

B. 1886     B. 1882     B.1871     B1878

Troedyrhiw        Abercanaid

| Tom | Dilys | Eluned | Mum | married | Dad | Walter | Harold | Bopa Liz | Maggie May |
|---|---|---|---|---|---|---|---|---|---|
| M. Vi | M. John Evans | mar. Emlyn Francis | Marion Peters | | Edward Mydrim | m. Peggy | m. Leah | m D.Williams | |
| | | | Born. 1911 | | Born 1906 | | | | |

Rhiwbina

| Len, Clive Michael | | Alun and Gwyn | Malcolm and Roderick | | | Marianne Glenda | Gillian and Gareth |
|---|---|---|---|---|---|---|---|
| | | twins 1944 | 1939 | 1944 | | 1933 | 1940    1942 |
| | | | married | married | | | |
| | | | Beverley | Mary John | | | |
| | | | | (Willicombe) | | | |

Pentyrch

| Tony, Alison, Leslie | Emlyn and Cathy | Ruth and Nathan | Jeremy and Sarah | Betty Willicombe | Tom and Netta John |
|---|---|---|---|---|---|
| | | | | (1927-1944) | 1898    1897 |

Dorothy

Lyndon, Raymond, Glen

Doris. Margaret and Glyn Willicombe

-------------------------------------------------------------------------------------------------------------(Mary's natural aunties and Uncle)

When I was a baby, can I remember my mother as I looked up from the pram? She had a lovely smile and wore a brown or was it a dark red coat? Perhaps something repetitive leads to a picture imprinted on my memory through the lenses of my eyes.

There's no doubt we were alike, Marion had wished for a girl but was saddled with another boy. Even so for the first four or five years of my life she was there and it seemed like just the two of us. She showed me how to pick the pieces of fluff off the stair carpet bit by bit so from a distance it looked as though the stairs had been vacuumed. Why did it mean so much to her to keep the house clean and tidy? For Eddie, her husband? Or maybe because it was a new house, a home that they'd moved into after they'd married in nineteen thirty-six.

We lived in Rhiwbina and I was born in Northlands, Cardiff in nineteen forty-four in a place run by nuns! There was no national health service at the time and with the war still in progress, and no immediate relatives around us I suppose my father thought it the safest place. My brother Malc had been born there five years earlier and up to then things must have seemed pretty rosy until the start of the Second World War. I always called him Malc as my father had done though in later years, he preferred Mac. At home my father called us 'titch and lightning' perhaps because Malc always tended to deliberated before he did anything. After my parents were married, they moved down from the Merthyr valley when my father had been offered a clerical job at Powel Dyffryn, Cardiff, the biggest private coal company in the country, and at the time he'd been working at the Plymouth Hill Colliery, Pentrebach.

I was born during a thunderstorm so she had said and that the midwife had named both Malcolm and me, at least she'd proposed the names but my second name, Courtland came from her father John Courtland Peters. Her relationship with him hadn't always been easy. He was English and her mother's family were deeply Welsh and he was blamed for the five children and the many miscarriages his wife Priscilla had suffered. At aged twenty he'd served with the Somerset Yeomanry in South Africa and then later he'd left Priscilla to fight in the First World War. But he had polished their shoes before school and carried her sewing machine to neighbouring villages when she became a seamstress, and had named her Marion after his sister who was three years older but didn't live to adulthood. Thomas, his son was named after his father then came Marion. The names of their other two daughters were his wife's choice, Eluned meaning image or idol and Dilys meaning sure and genuine. Another sister Joyce, had died in childhood from diphtheria a disease which had left Marion with a heart defect. I met someone at a wedding anniversary who had thought it quaint to see them in nineteen fifty walking hand in hand to a bench at the bottom of Elm Street, he was five feet nine and she barely five feet.

On seeing me for the first time jaundiced and with streaks of black hair she said "O ble gest ti fe?" From where did you have him? She suffered from severe asthma and died in nineteen fifty-three when I was nine years old. I can remember her using the kitchen table for support as she moved around the room refusing to let her condition defeat her. So much is said of the hardships men faced underground but more women were injured in the home than men in 'the pit' They were continually carrying boiling water from the fire to the 'bosh' or basin when accidents occurred, and there was the frequency of their dresses catching fire. The pressure on them to keep clothes clean in often large families, make food with often meagre rations was immense.Granch, my grandfather carried on living at his rented house in Elm Street until nineteen sixty-six working on his allotment and providing us with sacks full of potatoes. He would come to visit us in Porthamal Road and I remember waiting at the bay-fronted window with my mother until we could see him appear at the top of the road then she would let me out to run up the road to meet him. By the end he was deaf but would enjoy reading western, cowboy novels which he would read with the aid of a magnifying glass, in a room that was filled with the pungent smell of his pipe. Perhaps he was back in South Africa or in the Middle East in the First World War. Almost every Sunday we travelled to Merthyr. Aunty Flo next door (not a real aunty) would ask my mother if she was going 'home'. Yes. We would drop her off in Troedyrhiw with two apple tarts which she'd made for him before travelling another two miles to Abercanaid. I saw Granch last in nineteen sixty-six the year he died and as we said goodbye at his door he said "You look after her boy!" He was referring to Mary who was about to give birth to Sarah.

He had enlisted in the Royal Field Artillery almost immediately at the outbreak of World War One and at the age of thirty-two he could have perhaps been considered as too old, but it seems that he was anxious to leave what was a hard and difficult life as a collier without perhaps thinking of how it would affect Prescilla. His fellow miners were destined to go underground following their fathers at the age of fourteen, but his upbringing had been different. He was brought up in Jacobs Car Terrace in Bristol on the edge of Brandon Hill Park where he likely learned to ride and perhaps kept his horse which he needed to join the yeomanry. When I asked him what duties they were there to perform he told me that they were 'putting down a rebellion by the Zulus'. [The truth I suspect that he didn't even know was this. The British army had supplied their allies the Zulus with weapons to fight the Boar but when the British signed a peace treaty with the Boar they wanted them back, leaving the Zulus at the mercy of the Boar.] When he enlisted at twenty-one for South Africa he was described as a picture frame maker and could possibly have become a carpenter like his father had he not followed his brother to Merthyr on an ill-fated slaughterhouse scheme after leaving the yeomanry, and when it came to WW1 he could have been thought of as shirking his responsibilities since he did not arrive home until nineteen-twenty. His grandson Len remembers his father Thomas (Tom), having to leave school to find work quickly because the family were 'destitute'. An experience suffered by many. Tom continued in 'the pit' at Troedyrhiw playing football for the local team which at the time attracted a few thousand and more in attendance. He was obviously talented and after one game he was approached by someone from Llanharan who offered him accommodation and a job if he would play for them, as jobs were scarce, he accepted. My mother recalled one game that Tom played for Troedyrhiw when he wanted to look like a screen idol and swept his hair back with soap. Half way through the game it started to rain heavily and the soap ran into his eyes, thus Tom had to leave the field to wash the soap out. The cinema in Bridge Street, seemed to influence everyone from sayings my mother and her sisters used when they saw a handsome man. "Mama please buy me one of them" to fashions and hair styles. One detrimental effect was to do with teeth. My mother had perfectly healthy teeth but they were crooked and was persuaded to have them all removed so that her dentures would look perfect just like those actresses on the screen, and of course everyone smoked!

Also, in Troedyrhiw was Aunty Eluned (Lyn) and her husband Uncle Em. Emlyn Francis was a distinguished French horn player who played lead horn in the Birmingham Orchestra to rave reviews, one critic in nineteen-forty-four describing his playing as exceptional. He started from humble beginnings playing the euphonium as a teenager in the local brass band at Pentrebach when during a competition, a judge had recognised his talent and offered him a scholarship. He wasn't keen as it wasn't in his nature to leave home but his father insisted. On one occasion he'd arrived at the house unexpectedly feeling home-sick but his father had sent him back. What was the alternative a job in the mine?

In nineteen forty-four twins Alun and Gwyn were born and after the war had ended, they all returned home to Wales when Uncle Em secured a position in the BBC Welsh Orchestra living for a time in Rhiwbina then Troedyrhiw. After moving around the village, they settled down running the Glantaff Stores. Alun worshipped him and followed in his footsteps but he could not forgive his mother for her philandering. Whatever her reason she was promiscuous and it badly affected Uncle Em's nerves resulting eventually in him suffering a breakdown. She had scuppered Gwyn's chances of a relationship by insulting his long-term girl-friend something Alun might have challenged had it not been a time in his career when he had moved from horn playing to conducting eventually achieving success worldwide. Gwyn perhaps having something of his father's nature died a bachelor.

Aunty Dil would call once a week and I was surprised by the conversations that I overheard regarding Aunty Lyn and when I complained my mother would say "She's our sister and we say what we feel but if anyone else said anything woe betide them!" Little did I realize.

At Troedyrhiw was Aunty Jane my gran's sister who lived across the road from her and was always on the doorstep when we arrived. Next door was gran's brother, Uncle Ifan, a bachelor who Dilys and her husband John Evans had lived with after they were married. Dilys who was the most educated of the family had worked in accounts at Kaser Bonda and was a Sunday school teacher at Capel Nazareth where both Malc and me were christened. Later they bought a house in Tremorfa, Cardiff when they both began to work for BOAC at Maesycoed Road. As this was not far away, she would often visit, do my mother's hair and attempt to tutor me leading up to my Eleven-Plus examination. I say attempt because I vividly remember her very patiently explaining something to me and then asking me the answer to which I had no clue. To make matters worse I heard groans and tut tuts from mother and father who were also in the room. Why we hadn't conducted the lesson in the front room I'll never know. She was a lovely lady who lived up to her name but unfortunately, she'd inherited her mother's asthma and died in nineteen sixty-seven aged just forty-seven at Blackpool where the company had relocated.

Almost fifty years later I received a legacy from John Evan's second wife who had outlived him honouring Aunty Dil's wishes.

Abercanaid was a village which only had one road into it and that meant using a bridge over the river Taff which in the sixties was swept away leaving it cut-off until a temporary Bailey bridge was built by the army. Blaencanaid Farm was famous for holding the first nonconformist meetings but most of the early houses were built for colliers who worked in nearby mines one being the Gethin Pit where my grandfather, D'cu (Tadcu) and Uncle Walter worked for a short time. My great grandfather, Edward Thomas who came from Meidrim and who married for a second time looked after the fan in the Ventilation House for the Graig pit.

My grandmother Mam (Mamgu) lived at 55 Chapel Street and she had been a widow since nineteen forty-six when Thomas, D'cu had died. He had followed his father up from Meidrim where he'd been sent as a two-year-old when his mother, Elizabeth had died of small pox at Cwm Gwrach, near Resolven. It seems that D'cu had a much more religious education than his father at the Chapel in Meidrim where he had won many prizes, and it didn't help matters that Edward's second wife, Mary Bryant was Church of England. Edward and D'cu didn't mix much and to add to this situation Tomas Davis and his wife Margaret who had kept a farm, Penrhiw in Meidrim, where D'cu had worked, followed him to Abercanaid where they settled. He was very strict and was sometimes resented for his interference on one occasion putting his finger in a tear in Mamgu's apron making it worse and saying 'A stitch in time woman!' When Walter had spoken up against this he said 'You'll have trouble with him!' He's buried at Bancyfelin. 'Thomas Davis of Abercanaid.'

Top left my grandparents John Courtland Peters and Prescilla (Hughes).
Top right my grandparents Thomas Thomas and Sarah Jane (Walters).
Below Mum and Dad, Edward Mydrim Thomas and Marion (Peters),
then second generation Peters, Eluned (Lyn) Thomas, Dilys and Marion.

Alongside is Howard. Below trip to Craig y Nos arranged
by teacher John Jones extreme right, with Gus Saunders
next to him. Me, to the side and below the other teacher
extreme left with basin haircut and the Pollard twins below.
Bottom left Dad and Emlyn Lloyd. Alongside Wilf Lee at the
piano, John Thomas with 'moustache' and Dad behind him.

D'cu was brought up by his grandparents Thomas Thomas and his wife Rachel but was close to his great Aunt Esther who had married Jenkin Thomas of the Fountain Inn. He had made deliveries for them on a horse before reaching an age to work at Penrhiw farm. Esther died first and when Jenkin died, he left a share of his estate to D'cu. They are buried in Meidrim Church yard along with other members of the Thomas family. Their grave is marked with an obelisk.

Aunt Esther as a young woman had worked for her grandfather at the Wheaten Sheaf tavern which was once part of the village and one wonders if she had been responsible for, she and Jenkin buying and running the Fountain Inn.

D'cu worked for the Liverpool and Victoria insurance company and stood for the Liberal party in the late twenties but before going to election meetings my father and his brothers would want to know which language he would be speaking. If it was Welsh, they would sit with pride if English however, they would try to make themselves inconspicuous. The chapel played a large part in his life, he was a Precentor who rehearsed the congregation in readiness to perform at the Gamanfa or hymn singing festival and was also a Sunday school teacher. Something my father also did when he arrived at Rhiwbina.

Mam had good Welsh her parents coming from Llansadwrn near Llandovery and when she was too ill to go to the Graig Chapel on a Sunday evening, she would write sentences out in Welsh for me to learn. She died in nineteen fifty-eight of peritonitis. 55 Chapel Street was on the corner of Donald Street and living with Mam was her daughter Bopa Liz (aunty) and her husband Dick (Williams). A little way down Donald Street lived Maggie May, Liz's sister who was once married to a widower with children, almost a house keeper, she had been allowed to live out her days there after his death.

Uncle Walter was the eldest of the three brothers and lived at 1 Gethin Street where they kept a drapery shop. He had married Peggy who died in nineteen fifty-four. I can remember her making dough balls for us to go fishing with our make-shift rods in Webbers Pond. They had a daughter, Marianne Glenda who had come to stay with us in Rhiwbina when she was young. I remember riding on the back of Walters's motor bike when he would go out collecting instalments for the goods people had bought, and sleeping with him in a large double bed!

My father was the middle brother, then at the other end of the village at 1 Chapel Street lived Uncle Harold and his wife Leah and their two children Gareth and Gillian who were two and four years older than me respectively. During the summer holidays we'd stay with Mam then sometimes we'd stay with Harold where they had a small sweet shop in the front room. On those occasions it meant three in a bed with me stuck claustrophobically between Mac and Gareth. Harold had served in Burma and had a hatred of the Japanese after the things he'd seen there, and when he told me off for buying a Datsun car, I thought he was joking. But he was serious. He and an old comrade were going to cut down the flag pole which held the Japanese flag at the garage in Pentre Bach but ill health prevented them from doing it. He was a Christian until his dying day firstly attending Graig Methodist Chapel with the rest of the family then changing to the Baptists where his wife was a member. It did not seem to offend the rest of the family who willingly helped him during an election campaign in the early seventies when he stood for Plaid Cymru trying to secure a position on the council. His Welsh was good and he could converse easily in both languages with the electorate. Unfortunately, the ward wasn't ready to embrace Plaid Cymru.

Walter on the other hand had a hatred for religion and the Welsh language which he saw combined to stop the growth of the Welsh people. He probably disagreed with the narrowness he encountered in many chapel people and also their hypocrisy. There was also some truth in this which my father discovered first hand when he was sent underground during a miners' strike. There he met a deacon from the chapel, one my father had respected using "the foulest language he had ever heard!"

It's true that in the early days of Plaid Cymru some saw them as an elitist group and not the socialist party they were to become. Also, at the beginning the non-conformists would not even allow the use of a harmonium at their services and the playing of sport was frowned upon. Fortunately, this had disappeared and my father, a gifted soccer player had been spotted by Charlton where he'd had a trial but he made the decision not to go. The Abercanaid cricket team were one of the best in the league and won many trophies and there's a lovely photograph of the three brothers in the team celebrating an award. As for the harmonium by now the organ had been firmly established and according to Bopa Liz my father had become D'cu's favourite because he'd learnt how to play. Indeed, he'd first met my mother while playing at the children's Gamanfa at Nazareth. (I covered this in my short story Hidden Momentum). My father had cousins in the village the children of Mam's sister. Besse who had married a Griffiths, Lizzie Jane a fast-talking district nurse, and her sisters Violet and Florrie. Florrie had become a true friend when she had come down to live with us when my mother was ill. Violet had married a GI and lived on a farm in Kansas and had sent me 'real' cowboy-chaps when I was young. When she came over to visit in the seventies after her husband had died the brothers had hired a room in a pub where Lyndon and me played to the extended family. In the late seventies after Walter's funeral, she came with me when I visited Muriel Barry, the youngest of Edward's children with Mary Bryant in an attempt to find out more of the family but she couldn't add anymore. When Violet eventually came over here to live, they had moved to Swansea where the other side of their family lived but unfortunately, after a car crash Vi became bedridden.

Christmas was a special time when there were presents for everyone, usually money from Uncle Walter. Also, there was a tradition that when you wore a new suit for the first time, usually for the easter Gamanfa you were guaranteed some half-crowns from aunts and uncles! We'd go to the Sunday school at the chapel and read from the Bible in Welsh but concentrating on the pronunciation meant little room for understanding. Holidays were spent at the river field, playing hide and seek in the 'gwlis', lanes that seemed to run behind every house or in the grounds of the old library after first scaling the wall, and chips from the chip shop in Gethin street. On a Sunday evening Mamgu would cut bread perfectly holding the loaf to her breast and using a sharp knife, no serrated knives and no sliced bread. Coming home we counted the Christmas trees in the widows of the houses from Troedyrhiw to Whitchurch.

We travelled in Dad's car on what is now the old road to Merthyr taking a right at the lights at Old Church Road to Coryton, Tongwynlais, Taffs Well, Nantgarw, Upper Boat, Rhydyfelin, Glyntaff, Cilfynydd, Quakers Yard, Treharris, Edwardsville, Mount Pleasant, Merthyr Vale then Troedyrhiw. If my mother wanted to visit Gran and Joyce's grave, we would drop down to Aberfan which later contained Granch and Aunty Dil. I can remember using the bus with my mother, as Granch had done when visiting us but this meant a much longer journey. Dad's car belonged to the steel company where he worked for the rest of his life and was one of about three in the whole of the street. Dad was thirty-three when the war started and because he was responsible for obtaining and stocking coal to be made into coke for the making of steel his job was seen as a reserved occupation.

Because he was on the road day and night visiting collieries it occurred to one of the owners of Guest, Keen and Baldwin, a private company that he was ideally placed to evade the strict wartime conditions of the time and pick up a woman to be employed as a maid by the owner. On landing at Swansea, the woman spoke only in Irish which confused the customs people who left her alone. This gave Dad an opportunity to beckon her to him and through a small hole in a fence she and Dad made their escape. It was agreed that he should take her home and bring her into work the following day and so she slept in the 'box room'. The next morning there was a tap on the bedroom door and the maid brought them their breakfasts on trays. She announced that the fire was lit and asked for further instructions. My mother was so disappointed to have to tell her that this wasn't to be the house where she would work.

We also had a telephone, care of the steel works and one of the few in the street. It was only used by close friends until the news of it spread and as it was positioned in the hall it was hard not to hear people's conversations. One woman who'd been talking in English suddenly said 'We'll talk in Welsh now' to the annoyance of my mother. My mother only spoke in English but had a good knowledge of Welsh which my father would use when speaking to her if he wanted to keep something from us. As the woman left, leaving four pennies next to the phone my mother said 'Popeth yn iawn?' (Everything okay?) to which the woman who was taken aback answered 'Oh. Oh, yes. Diolch.'

My mother was happy being single and it seems that a certain amount of well-intentioned pressure by her mother and Aunty Dil, convinced her that a handsome man with good prospects was someone she should seriously think about and when Dilys sang in the children's Gamanfa, and my father had accompanied her on the organ they had met. She had worked firstly in a London hospital where Aunty Lyn had been a nurse before joining an outdoor advertising team who knocked on doors across the country promoting various products and giving away free samples. Before television, this was the only way to inform people apart from cinema trailers, newspaper advertising and Radio Luxembourg which began transmitting in nineteen thirty-three.

From the time I can remember until I was ten years old, we spent our two-week summer holiday at Weston Super Mare where we stayed with (Auntie) Min a lady that my mother had lodged with during her life in advertising. On one of these holidays my cousin Marianne Glenda was getting married and Mum and Dad took the Paddle Steamer from the old pier at Weston to Cardiff which was far easier than travelling by car around Gloucester or taking 'pot luck' on the Aust Ferry, and they were back later that evening.

Mum found marriage a challenge especially after rowing with Mrs Oram next door, over something that happened before I was born, and no amount of coaxing by Jeff Read's mum (my childhood friend) or aunty Flo, next door, could persuade her to relent. Later on, I must have made life difficult for her when I insisted on helping Mr Oram build his garage. Help being the wrong word as I was six but he humoured me and some five years later he showed me some chords on his ukulele, which I had been learning, this took place in the back garden!

Life must have seemed lonely at times and she would spend her time making dresses. While working she had altered her uniform which she had felt dated and was soon responsible for changing the uniforms of the other girls once they saw it. On the occasions my mother would visit Abercanaid she would be popular with Marianne Glenda and Gillian because of the clothes she wore and later she could taper trousers for me and Gwyn expertly unlike my friend Howard who unfortunately looked as though he wore 'jodhpurs'. The Rockets skiffle group proudly wore red shirts emblazoned with a white rocket.

Mum didn't mix easily; she wasn't a member of Beulah Church like my father and if we went on an outing with the church to Langland or Caswell Bay, we would sit apart from the others even though they would ask her to join them. Living in Rhiwbina meant conforming and I remember coming home from junior school to find a tramp sitting on a dining room chair on the path outside of the front door with a cup of tea and a sandwich. She'd felt sympathy for him and perhaps remembered her life on the road in advertising and so this was the way she had to do it without being compromised.

She began sketching the cat in various positions and later introduced colour using my brother's-coloured pencils. When I inherited these my class-mates were amused to see them labelled with red, for instance written on paper and sellotaped to the red pencil! This was done because Mac was colour blind but he had no trouble with red, it was the subtler greens, brown and maroons that he had trouble distinguishing. My mother then started to use water colours and I remember being particularly impressed by a snow scene of our back garden and garage, next was a still life, a bowl of fruit with the wall-paper in the background. With this I'm ashamed to say she entered a competition under my name and won a prize! She became more comfortable when Betty Gent arrived who being Scottish welcomed them on New Year's Eve, the Lloyds and brother and sister-in-law would arrive for a meal over Christmas and there were Dad's steel works, Christmas dances. She liked a drink unlike my father who was a shandy man, and often I walked Lil Buttle home after she and Mum had had a drink. In her fifties she met Gwen Goodliffe and together they went to art lessons at Whitchurch Sec., and as a result she spent much of her time painting in oils.

Our gang consisted of Jeff, Keith Lane, David Muxworthy, Graham Beer, Mike Evans, Phil Jones and Ros his younger sister who would also tag along. During the summer holidays Pasha, a mild-mannered Alsatian would join us, his owners telling my mother how he missed us when we started back to school. When he died, we felt as though we'd lost a member of our group.

At the bottom of Porthamal Road was Hill-Snook Park and to the right was the 'horses' field', now part of the park. To the left was a lane that led to a bridge over the Cardiff Railway line and on the other side to the left was Cardiff Corries football ground and to the right a discarded field. We made dens in the Japanese Knot-wood which must have grown to six foot in height and further over towards Waun Gron Avenue under-ground dens. This was done by digging out the den, covering it with zinc sheets and placing turf on top.

Les Read, Jeff's father built us one at the top his garden which had sliding doors, probably out of an old kitchen. We must have been about five when we used this because during a game of 'I'll show you mine if you show me yours' with an obliging girl of the same age Jeff burned my 'pecka' with a match or candle used to light the den. When my mother bathed me that evening, I gritted my teeth as I sank into the water.

The lane ran up to Beulah Road and at the time was the boundary between Cardiff City council on the right and Cardiff Rural District council on the left which meant among other things a different catchment area for schools.

Rhiwbina for instance was allied to Whitchurch, Tongwynlais, Capel Llanilltern, Pentyrch, Radyr and Morganstown. We'd cross Beulah Road into Heol y Felin and at the end of the road near the Butchers Arms cross the style and into the fields which ran to Thornhill and on to Caerphilly Common perhaps crossing a minor B road on the way. Often, we'd set out to find the source of the Rhydwaedlyd stream on the way passing the field where Beulah Congregational Church would have their Whitson Treats at Thornhill. Starting early in the morning on the day of the Whitson Treat everyone would meet at the Assembly Rooms and chairs, trestle-tables and tents would be loaded onto flat-bed lorries and taken up to the freshly mowed field. I suppose we were more of a hindrance than a help. On another occasion we found clay in the banks of the stream and brought half a sackful back on a 'bogie' with great ideas of modelling something, but alas we didn't know then that it had to be sieved and washed to purify it first.

In primary school Gareth Saunders' father was an art teacher at Cathays High School and was also a keen naturalist and could often be heard on Radio Wales talking about the birds and plants he'd seen at various times of the year. At his home in Wenallt Road he had a goshawk that he'd trained to hunt and it would fly the length of the garden and then return to his arm, Gus' arm or mine. He also had a small flock of sheep on a field above the Graig Goch valley at the top of Rhiwbina hill and we decided it would be an ideal place to camp out.

So, at about nine- or ten-years old Gus, Geoff Robbins, Derek Allcock and me set out with a tent my father had acquired some years before with US Army stencilled on the side and the canvas material meant that if you brushed against the inside of the tent, you could create a drip which you had to put up with until more clement weather dried it out. Gus was well on the way to being a 'country man' and he knew much about the fields and woods around, he'd pick up a furry ball beneath a tree which he called an owl's pellet and as he opened it, he described the fur and bones that the owl couldn't digest and had discarded. One evening when our fire was almost out a rabbit appeared in the hedgerow and we tried to tempt it by throwing pieces of bread to it but the rabbit seemed oblivious and eventually as it got nearer Gus picked it up, but to our horror we found it was blind and had an enlarged head. Instinctively Gus kicked it in the air killing it. It had myxomatoses the disease which had been intentionally inoculated into wild rabbits in France and was here by 1953.

The weather was quite miserable and Derek, who had arrived in a T shirt and shorts spent most of his time in the tent reading comics and helping himself from the box of supplies which were situated in the triangular end of the tent. It rankled, so when he left the tent to pee, I couldn't resist shooting him in the bottom with the air pistol we had. It was very low powered but he did dance around for a while until his pain subsided.

Geoff then pierced his hand while trying to open a tin of beans and because he was clearly in pain he decided to go home. It was dusk by the time we left, as I accompanied him the half a mile or so from the field and along the lane until we reached Rhiwbina hill and then down to the Deri and the bus stop. Geoff lived at the top of Porthamal Road so I walked on down to my house surprising my parents. I was happy to return and my father took me back up to Rhiwbina hill in his car and left me at the entrance to the lane but now I had a torch which made things much easier. When I reached the tent, I made threatening bull-type noises outside the tent and giggled at the panic I'd caused inside until the airgun poked out through the flap of the tent, the lead pellet narrowly missing my ear. We collected our water from the Cwm Nofydd stream which ran through the bottom of the valley and to get to it we had to negotiate a steeply wooded slope. Imagine our surprise to see the old lady who lived in a cottage at the beginning of the lane down at the stream collecting her water and politely refusing all our offers of help.

I inherited a strong Welsh accent from my mother who seemed to live for her visit to Troedyrhiw at weekends. My father also had quite a strong accent when he relaxed at home but it changed immediately, when he answered the phone and like most people, he altered it to suit his surroundings. He was happiest with John Thomas or Emlyn Lloyd who lived in Landsdown Avenue but was originally from Merthyr, and they both belonged to a Welsh concert party called Cwmni Wenallt who would often rehearse in our house. He would speak Welsh with them and sometimes to my mother who understood but rarely spoke it. I felt safe and contented at home and I didn't really like junior school whereas brother Mac easily became a citizen of Rhiwbina and the world. When he was in his last year at junior school and I was in primary, I would go to his classroom so that he could take me home and when I entered the boys would say 'come and sit with me' in chorus to the annoyance of Miss Foster.

Music was always around us but the first time I ever felt a buzz from making music was when I was about ten years old and met Clive Roderick at Rhiwbina Junior School. He lived in a large detached house with his mother and younger sister and seemed to want for nothing, and when invited to parties the atmosphere was far more relaxed, and even girls were invited! Something I wouldn't have dreamt of asking of my parents. I don't know when he arrived at the school and we weren't in the same class but we became friends and had 'girlfriends' twins, Sally and Wendy Pollard from Ty'n y Parc Road. I put the memories of that 'far off place' in a song titled School Photograph which applied to me and friend Howard if not to Clive.

'Short hair short pants we were about short of everything, Grey socks stained ties chapped thighs touch them and how they'd sting, Tree dens scraped shins wars that ended when it was time to go in, School trips soft lips and love affairs you only knew how to begin, Promises made in the playtime sun she told me that I'd always be the one, If I saw her today oh how we'd laugh, laugh, laugh, But see how she smiles on my school photograph'

His father it appeared had been a successful business man but how long he'd been dead when we met, I didn't know. My father could remember him when they were in the Home Guard together. At one point they had a manoeuvre to 'take' the village hall at Tongwynlais some three miles away on a wet and windy night. Tom Roderick brought his car around and Dad and his friends jumped in much against the ethos of the Home Guard. But as our friendship developed, I found that if Clive didn't want to talk about something he didn't. Even requests by his mother or teachers fell on deaf ears. It was his father I'm fairly sure who had taught him a few chords on the ukulele and when he taught them to me, I wanted to learn more and at the next opportunity, at Christmas I had my own instrument and we began to play regularly together. One teacher heard us and thought we could bring something extra to the school choir performance and so it was, Clive and me would play during Lawr Ar Lan y Mor each standing either side of the stage.

There was always music at home. My mother would either have the radio on or would play her records while she worked. The radio, the Light Programme as it was then could play anything from 'novelty' records, pop of the day, Johnnie Ray or Frankie Lain to classical pieces. Among her records were those of Dvorak, Holst and Ravel and I remember her explaining to me one afternoon that we were going to listen to Uncle Em, who was about to play Mozart's Horn Concerto with the

BBC Orchestra, which was being broadcast on the radio.

When Dad got home from work, he would regularly go into the front room where he'd play the piano as if to unwind while Mum prepared the evening meal. The piano had replaced a pedal organ which my father favoured and which he'd played during chapel services in Abercanaid and beyond before moving with Mum to work in Cardiff. He thought that if firstly my brother Mac and then me were to learn music then a piano was the best instrument. Unfortunately, neither of us could keep to the discipline of lessons and practice though Mac showed more aptitude.

At about aged nine, before meeting Clive, I remember distinctly being in trouble with my father because my teacher, who knew my father had told him that he thought my soprano voice was good enough to win the school Eisteddfod but that I didn't respond to his encouragement. Was I shy? Did I not want to put myself out there I don't know but once the episode had passed, I spent many evenings standing alongside my father at the piano learning songs such as All in The April Evening and Pistyll y Llan which I then went on to perform at local concerts. One performance was in Beulah Church when I had to climb a narrow passage to arrive at the side of the organ at a certain point during the service and sing. The organist, Wilf Lee was a lovely man who worked in the ROF Factory but sadly died only a few years later. It was a moment of realisation of the closeness of death and when I met his son who I knew, though not well I remember feeling his pain but failed to find the words to sympathise. Ironically the song I sang was Come unto Him by Handel.

The Assembly Rooms at Beulah was the perfect setting for youth clubs, junior and senior and with a main hall and stage the drama society regularly performed their plays. From the late forty's concerts and 'gang shows' were produced one of them, Gentleman's Evening, being the most popular where, as the name suggests all the participants were men from the church. The entertainment consisted of songs and comic sketches one of which for some reason particularly upset me seeing my father as a patient, and John Thomas operating on him and pulling all manner of things, like a string of sausages from his stomach. John was the epitome of a villain from a melodrama with flashing eyes and a thick black moustache and it took me some time to realise he was only acting. In the early fifties and in another show, they sang a cowboy song with Dad wearing my hat perched on his head and wielding my toy pistol while John had a perfectly fitting Stetson hat and a Colt 45 which he proceeded to fire at the end of the song deafening the first three rows and filling the hall with smoke. His interest in the Wild West didn't diminish and when we visited him in the seventies at Sealyham Home Farm in Letterston, he stated that Tom Mix had attended Wyatt Earp's funeral thus the movie star had acknowledged a legitimate legend of the west. Joan, John's wife told us of how, on hearing the Jimmy Webb song By The Time I Get To Phoenix he had spread a map of the USA on the table and followed the towns and cities mentioned in the song. At another concert entitled Thomas' Night Dad sang Let My People Go and the duet The Gendarmes with John and all recorded on his new Philips tape recorder.

The tape recorder was only three and three-quarters in speed but punched way above its weight when it came to recording everything from concerts, which I managed to transfer to CD, or to its use in the home. Dad would also record conversations when friends came for a meal, but unbeknown to them, then play it back to them as entertainment. On the tape Mary Lloyd asked where we were my mother replied that Mac was upstairs doing his homework and me, who'd also been told to stay in had said 'bugger him' and gone out. Even my father had laughed at this. In Abercanaid Uncle Walter had bought the same model and recorded Marianne Glenda singing a nice version of Softly by Ruby Murry, then one evening at 55 Chapel Street the tape wound itself around the spindle and eventually as the night wore on, and with Mum wondering where we were, it was cut out with a knife and scissors.

In 1955 I started at Whitchurch Secondary Modern school after failing my Eleven Plus examination and met Howard Clements who was to be my friend until his death in 2018. He was from a similar background to me his parents moving to Whitchurch from the Rhondda and he also had a good soprano voice, which was better than mine having a kind of tenor quality and we sang against each other in school Eisteddfodau. I have a snatch of us on tape/CD singing Little Brown Jug which my father had recorded in the front room.

Academically we found ourselves in the top stream which meant that we were destined to take O Levels, Auntie Dilys' tuition had not all been in vain, and which of course was the model for the Comprehensive system to come.

Clive also started at the school which surprised me because children from the more affluent homes who had failed, had been sent to private schools, but then he did what he wanted to do and perhaps our friendship meant something to him. So, the three of us became firm friends for the next five years even when Clive decided he didn't want to take O Levels. Friends in school and at his home at Heol Wen. His mother always seemed to be out somewhere and we took advantage of the available alcohol which was on hand and which for Howard and me was a great attraction, and when she was away, we stayed over. One day I had a fight in the village, which fortunately I won but instead of saying nothing he bragged to his mother who banned me for a while until he had insisted that I carry on as his friend.

At Whitchurch in our first year, we met Dave Reynolds who was our art teacher but also played the guitar and when he saw us playing ukuleles, he involved us in a group of pupils that he was taking to Dyffryn House. His idea was to show teachers how the guitar could be used in schools and with some older pupils we performed some folk songs with Clive and me accompanying another pupil playing a melody on a guitar. Reynolds's art had appeared on the Welsh language programme Hop Y Deri Dando where he sang and played and quite soon, my father had 'roped him in' to perform with Cwmni Wenallt and on one occasion after a long bus ride to Llandovery he, and Clive and me were involved in the show. He took an interest in Clive and wanted him to take O Level art even after he'd dropped out and because we were keen to learn more of the guitar and spent some time with him, he must have realised that Clive's father was dead. But it wasn't in

Clive's nature to need anyone.

In April 1957 when I was almost thirteen, I went into Cardiff Royal Infirmary to have my appendix out. Mac had hurt his ankle playing football and Dad was taking him to the doctors when Mum said "take tich with you for heaven's sake". And so, I ended up in hospital. In fairness to her if anything was psychosomatic it was my appendix! Mac had had his out and I was either a witness to this or he had told me about it, no doubt embellishing every detail, so that I was terrified of it happening to me. I spent two weeks there, which was normal in those days and one day a nurse took me to a room where two doctors were playing guitars, the song was Singing The Blues which was released by Tommy Steele in the January and though I could play it on the ukulele I was determined to learn more of the guitar when I got back home. In the November of that year That'll Be The Day by the Crickets was released and I dearly wanted an electric guitar but Dad, in his wisdom bought me a banjo! Which I then used to accompany Cwmni Wenallt, standing alongside Merfyn on the piano. That was dad's ulterior motive, I'm sure!

Our annual holiday consisted of two weeks usually in Bournemouth or Newquay, Cornwall when my father would make sure the banjo and guitar were stowed in the boot and we'd invariably be asked to sing at the place we stayed and also enter the talent shows which were popular at that time.

In nineteen fifty-seven also we heard Bye Bye Love by the Everly Brothers and began to sing it. We both had an ear for harmony listening to our father and having had to learn different parts for singing hymn tunes particularly for the Children's Gamanfa singing festivals. It was Mac who worked on the harmonies. Listen to At The Hop* Skiffle however was still the driving force and we were soon joined by Clive Seddon on washboard and vocals, a friend from Beulah Youth Club, his cousin, Graham Parsonage on guitar and one of Mac's friends Steve Grey on vocal harmonies and tea-chest bass. We seemed to be out playing every weekend but at thirteen years of age I took no part in organising gigs or practices in the front room. Mac and Steve were almost eighteen at the time, Clive was sixteen and Graham fifteen.

I can only remember those 'gigs' that for some reason have stayed in my mind. A photograph of us at a Rhiwbina fête* where we met Roy Galpin for the first time and who later provided some amplification for us. Roy and his brother had a shop in Beulah Road selling TV's and radios and Roy spent most of his time installing or repairing equipment. Playing on the back of a flat-bet lorry at Llanishen sticks in my mind, my fingers stinging as I tried to hold down a chord in the cold air.

The song Jesse James was recorded by Lonnie Donegan and was one which we made our own. I sang the verses with Mac and Steve providing the harmonies on the chorus then Clive would recite a verse in the way of a cowboy ballad. It must have been quite effective because in early fifty-eight we won a Cardiff Youth Clubs competition with it and an Eisteddfod held at the Hoover Social Club in Merthyr Tudful. This competition was advertised for entrants from Merthyr a'r

Cylch meaning those from the district so it was something of a stretch to include us from Rhiwbina.

How this was allowed I do not know but obviously had something to do with the fact that my father had been born and bred in the village of Abercanaid across the river and that my grandmother, two aunties, two uncles, three cousins and other relations still lived there. I remember feeling a certain animosity from the other competitors and when I realised that I had the strongest Welsh accent, while the others including my brother had what I suppose was a Cardiff suburbs accent which must have rankled with our rivals. To add to my embarrassment when we took part in the heats in the afternoon, I met my cousins, Alun and Gwyn who lived only few miles down the road. They had a similar line up to ours but perhaps weren't quite as polished and they had spent some time on their hill-billy costumes complete with false beards.

This probably didn't endear them to the organisers who had described the Eisteddfod as a Jazz and Folk Song Competition and the costumes were maybe felt inapt so they didn't get through. There were some awkward moments for a few weeks after the event which my poor mother experienced mostly from her sister, but eventually it was forgotten. After the heats we were fed and thoroughly spoilt by my aunties and then played football on the river-field in Abercanaid.

I don't remember our winning performance as it was probably much like others but back in Abercanaid my Uncle Walter took us to the pubs in the village where we performed. We had another friend of my brothers, John Downing who played a bass drum and snare with us and squeezing those into one of the pubs proved a challenge.

We came home later that night by train my father presumably taking the instruments in his car. Clive Seddon was tipsy and happy and I liked his carefree attitude and from then on, I picked up his ways especially the easy way in which he befriended girls and realised that performing on stage had its advantages. We played a few times in Merthyr and on a photograph* of us at the Miners Hall I remember a girl leaning on the stage when I was singing and rubbing her finger gently 'round my shoe! On the photo we're playing behind permanently fixed music stands which reminds me of playing at Cardiff City Hall during the band's intermission and loading up Dad's car under the halls elaborate porch in the rain.

That was perhaps one of the last times we sang The Ballad of Jesse James except by me on stage during a schools Eisteddfod though we did make a record and included it with other songs including At The Hop which we recorded in our front room. Also, on it is my first attempt at song writing. The less said!

We were asked to play at Craig y Parc in Pentyrch which was a school for children with physical disabilities by the deputy headmaster, John Jones. He had been my teacher at Rhiwbina and was responsible for our trip to Madam Patti's castle, Craig y Nos which had become a hospital for those convalescing from TB. On a small stage our choir sang into a microphone which was relayed to the wards. Later at Craig y Parc our skiffle group played in a large summer-house with a thatched roof and at the end of the night the children were taken one by one to their beds. We couldn't quite understand what one boy was telling us as he pointed to the roof until we realised that it was on fire. The children then had an exciting end to the evening as they watched the fire-brigade deal with the now empty summer-house.

That'll Be The Day by Buddy Holly and the Crickets became the biggest musical influence in my life first hearing it, Mac and me, listening to Radio Luxembourg on a portable radio in the front room. Tuning in was a nightmare but reception seemed better at night and after buying the single I waited in anticipation for the next releases, Peggy Sue, It's So Easy, Rave On and the softer Take Your Time, Heartbeat and Words Of Love. In nineteen-fifty-eight Mary bought me the album and those songs became the backing track to my life and there, in the front room of Heol-Danyrodyn, I didn't realise then that I was falling in love with her.

Both Howard and Clive had shown an interest in her while I was happy in the band and meeting other girls. Howard once wrote a story about me saying that I was ahead of them, worldly wise so to speak and I do remember my father grabbing me one day while on holiday and shaving off my moustache.

We played at a youth-club dance and afterwards I walked a girl home to the house she was staying at in Rhiwbina while taking a course in domestic science. I was fifteen and she was seventeen. I must have been so full of myself. To make matters worse I had to knock my father up out of bed and I received a severe outburst, Mac had been home some hours before. There was Caroline who was my girlfriend and partner at the Memorial Hall dances and was much nearer to home than Pentyrch. Her father who I never met kept a revolver complete with bullets in a drawer in his bedroom and when I saw it that made me think twice about deceiving her, but eventually deceive her I did. After leaving Rhiwbina junior school she had gone to Our Ladies Convent school, Cardiff where Sally Hamlin, the girl Mac was going out with also went and we were both the subject of much gossip when they realised this. Our last holiday as a family was at Bournemouth where I met Cynthia a delightful seventeen-year-old from Llanelli who among other things taught me the correct way to French-Kiss. One of the other guests at the hotel had seen us in the sea and stated that she could tell when two young people wanted to be alone, much to my embarrassment. Later she wrote to me, the letters I carefully hid in the back of the piano but not carefully enough. I arrived home from school one day to find my mother had discovered them and because they could have been considered intimate, I was banned from continuing any other correspondence. Apart from playing rugby for the school both Mary and I were in the athletics team as runners, sprinters, one teacher from another school describing us as affectionate twins! When we took part in a meeting at Maindy Stadium the day seemed to go on for ever so we decided to go to the Plaza Cinema which wasn't too far away. Unbeknown to us the relay team which Mary was part of had reached the finals but she was nowhere to be found. The next morning poor Mary had a dressing-down on stage during assembly. Perhaps this had something to do with her decision to leave and so at fifteen, much to the annoyance of teachers and the headmistress who were expecting her to take O Levels Mary left school.

She could easily persuade her parents and as she had already secured a position in an accounts department of a furniture store it was settled. There was a girl in my year who I saw briefly until Jean Curtis, Mary's best friend accused me of three-timing! Clive who had also left school had ingratiated himself with her by blackening my name which I suppose was justified so at almost sixteen I started to see her again sometimes skipping school if I knew she was at home and for the first time I knew that I was in love with her. We'd fumbled our way through love making a year before and this had created a bond that would last the rest of our lives.

By this time, I'd lost interest in school-work and was surprised when Howard phoned from the Western Mail Offices to say I'd passed five O levels, the same as him. This was his second call the first one was to tell me, excitedly that he'd lost his virginity! He'd been dating a girl who at first had shown little interest in him but he'd persevered and his sense of humour and chat-up lines taken directly from the screen had proved successful. A year later he went up for an audition at RADA and though he had a good audition he decided to pass his A-Levels before committing himself and consequently his dream faded.

There was pressure put on me by the metalwork teacher and the woodwork teacher with who I was particularly friendly to retake English in the November and become a craft teacher but I wanted to get a job, earn money and grow up as fast as I could. During my last year in school, I delivered meat on a butcher's bike for George Raybould as Mac had done some years before. He was a good payer which I didn't realize until Howard and me were comparing our 'wages' one day. Howard was delivering groceries for the Coop next door. This meant that Mary didn't always have to pay when we went to the Monico cinema. On a Friday evening I'd chop-up large pieces of fat then mince the fat down into a vat with a tap on it, then heat it up on a gas ring in the shed outside ready to fill bags emblazoned with a cow, after I'd finished my round. He'd then sell the bags as dripping. For some reason I was doing this on a Saturday morning when I chopped my fingers with a meat axe. George was talking to me at the time and drinking a cup of tea which exploded out of his mouth when he realised what I had done. The lady in the shop next-door which belonged to George's brother bandaged me up and afterwards I marked out the football pitch with whitewash. My parents had been to a wedding and when they got home that evening, I was back down the Infirmary having a couple of stitches. Needless to say, George felt the rough end of my mother's tongue when he called in. This was something he did most Saturdays after a Rhiwbina Athletic game as he was manager and my father treasurer. Mac played for the senior team and was really talented and could easily have played in the Welsh league had he taken up their offers. I got by in the under eighteens side though soccer wasn't really my game though I did play for Troedyrhiw. It happened when I went with Dad to support Mac who was having a trial with them only to find the team was short of players and I was asked to play also. I had no kit so they found me a pair of boots from the forties or even earlier and at the end of the game both my big toes throbbed which even the ten shillings passed to me in an envelope couldn't ease. Over the next few months both toenails turned black and then and eventually fell off!

So, back in fifty-nine I picked up a second-hand guitar, acoustic of course as electric guitars were out of our price range, Mac tuned the bottom strings down on his guitar and with a pick-up fitted played a 'kind of' bass using the radio as an amplifier to begin with then later a guitar amp.

Clive switched from washboard to drums and we found we could do a reasonable imitation of the Crickets vocally that is, except of course for Buddy's voice and the Stratocaster guitar. It wasn't until later that we discovered that the actual background vocals were not supplied by the Crickets but by backing singers such as the Picks and June Clark and Gary & Ramona Tollett.

So now we became a rock and roll group but because of our lack of electric instruments we were firmly in the vocal group camp but we continued to be asked to play particularly at the Rhiwbina Memorial Hall Teenage Dance Club. Clive Roderick would sometimes join us and after seeing us playing he immediately bought himself an electric guitar (a Tuxedo) and an amplifier. He could play well but he was unreliable.

He always joined me however when I set out at night to scour the building sites in search of a piece of wood out of which I could make an electric guitar. After a few attempts I made one. The first was a semi acoustic with F holes which I partially built, but was still in the school woodwork store room long after I left. The second attempt was a solid more basic effort and when I fitted a pick-up it had a surprisingly good sound and though I had to use a capo to compensate for some defect I played it for the next four years.

In nineteen-sixty I started my apprenticeship as an electrician in the steel works, and was spending more time with Mary. Mac was in his second year of accountancy; Steve had gone off to college and Graham had joined the Navy.

About this time Mac went on a cruise with Sally Hamlin and her family and she commented how quaint was the way Mac 'bashed' the crusts on the toast he'd made for her something my mother had always done probably back to the story of teeth!

We played at the Hamlin's house and a friend of Mr. Hamlin came up from the docks to play with us and turned out to be a really good jazz guitarist. Though it wasn't strictly our kind of music we joined in and enjoyed the experience.

Later Clive Seddon told me that Mr Hamlin wanted to manage us, something I Obviously missed but Mac, for some reason didn't want to involve him.

Mac and me in the backyard of Porthamal Road.

Outside Aunty Min's in Western Super Mare.

Mary with Netta and Tom.

A family holiday. Mum, Dad, me and Mac behind.

Malc playing for Rhiwbina Athletic.

Mary and me at Newquay, Cornwall 1960-61.

This is either the Miners Hall Merthyr or the City Hall, Cardiff during the band's break. We must have been singing Jesse James with Clive Seddon 'speaking' his verse

The guitar made from a piece of wood filched from a building site. The hardest part I seem to remember was the fret board. This the back garden of Porthamal Road with me singing into a broom and my guitar plugged into an orange box. That was Mac's sense of humour.

This was a Christmas dance at St. Mellon's Country Club. This must have been just before Lyndon joined us. Mac has Clive Roderick's Tuxedo guitar on his lap which I must have borrowed for the occasion.

The following summer Mary and me went to Newquay, Cornwall together with another couple, Marilyn and John. My father had thoughtfully made sure that we had a reserved compartment and at our journeys end we stayed with the same people where I had stayed with Mum and Dad two years before. We really enjoyed being in each other's company without the dreaded 'it's time to go home' and even though the other couple didn't get on and I had sun-stroke for a few days it was hard to say goodbye at the end of the holiday.

Netta John was forty-eight when she adopted Mary after her mother had died aged seventeen, her father being a GI stationed at Rhydlafar a mile from the village. This had annoyed her mother's natural sister Doris who was the eldest of three with Margaret and Glyn who were still in school. She had arranged for her to be adopted by a well-off family but Netta who had delivered both Mary and her mother won out. Mary's grandfather also wanted her kept in the village and with two families there, John and Willicombe, her grandfather's name, she grew up often being called Betty, her mother's name by mistake. They lived at Temperance Road together with Netta's daughter, Dorothy and when she got married, she and her husband Albie also came there to live. Their son Lyndon was born there in nineteen-forty-six before they moved to Gwaelod y Garth in nineteen-fifty. Netta, Tom and Mary moved to a brand-new council house in nineteen fifty-seven at 15 Heol Danyrodyn where I would be invited to tea and it would become, though I didn't know it then a part of my life for the next five years. Pentyrch was a small village which only contained about two hundred houses and it was not on any through route so you needed a specific reason to go there. It also had a 'closeness' about it as most people were the descendants of those who had gone before. In nineteen-sixty-one I played for a season with Pentyrch youth with boys I'd been in school with. Based at Mary's house I got off the bus, to see Norman Follis, who was blind about to walk down Heol y Pentre to the house where he lived. I'd noticed that if someone else was walking that way they'd say "Going down Norm?" to which he'd link his arm in theirs thereby avoiding any obstacles on the way. I walked up along-side him and asked if he was going down to which he linked his arm in mine and said "Mary John's boyfriend is it?"

We walked the lanes in the snow at winter time and down to Rhydlafar Hospital at the height of summer usually to visit Tom who stoked the boiler which provided hot water and heating for the hospital. The Nissen-huts were still there where the American medics had been stationed but had been used later by families without homes. Because of a shortage of houses after the war, these people who were actually squatters were allowed to live there until council houses were built to accommodate them. The children had gone to school in Pentyrch and Mary remembered going to many a birthday party there.

Each year the carnival, which ran for a week would be held in the village with a fun-fair set up at the rugby field. There would be entertainment each night of the week one being the teenage dance where we played on the stage of St Catwgs Church Hall. For a short while I seemed to lose her when Jean's parents who enjoyed Tom and Netta's company suggested she and Jean should see more of each other. They lived at Pantmawr Road, Rhiwbina and when I walked across the golf course to see her, I found they'd befriended guys with motor bikes and for a moment I felt outclassed so I decided to get one, but my parents would have none of it. The compromise was a Bond-mini car.

This was a three wheeled fibre-glassed bodied car with a two-fifty cc motor cycle engine perched on the front wheel and at seventeen I could drive it with a provisional motor-cycle license without a competent driver alongside me.

That was the theory until I took my test, which I failed after arguing with the examiner. Clive had a Berkley car which had the third wheel at the back. So, at last I had some form of independence and I could leave the steel works for home or Pentyrch but the car could be unreliable. The car had an electric start by turning a key but that soon broke down and I was reduced to opening the bonnet placing my foot inside where I 'kick-started' the engine. I left work at four on a weekday and unbeknown to me I was a great source of entertainment to those who worked in an office block opposite who would gather at their window to watch me 'kick' the car into life. I worked on a lathe in the trade school for a while and the 'wag' next to me kept me entertained with stories. He was older than me and one day he announced that he'd passed his exam, he'd got picked for the first team and his girlfriend had had her period and he was happy. Little did I realise how my life would change. The year progressed and my apprenticeship stipulated that I attend Llandaff Technical college sometimes one day a week and sometimes block release which meant spending a month in college at a time. The company paid for this as long as you passed your exams and for the first three years, I didn't find this a problem. The band didn't play quite as much but now we were more professional. Mac had an electric bass and amplifier my home-made guitar did the job with a guitar amp and Lyndon, Mary's nephew joined Mac on backing vocals. Roy Galpin was still a friend and would set up a PA for us if one wasn't available at the venue and one night when the PA went down at the Scout's Hall in Rhiwbina, I turned to see him at the back of the stage with his amp in pieces! Only to discover that someone had inadvertently switched the power off to it! Roy was something of a boffin insisting on buying his round of drinks at the Lewis Arms one night with five- and ten-pound notes flying everywhere where he'd stuffed them in his pocket. At the gig at the Scouts Hall, I saw someone flick a cigarette end into the air without any thought of where it would land and thinking of the lacquer that girls used in their hair and the fact that Mary was in the audience I stopped and pointed at him making sure he could see me. When he and his friend approached the stage, I knelt down and gave him a piece of my mind but it fell on deaf ears so I stood up and took off my guitar intending to take it further. Lyndon's friends had come down to see us perform and were standing at the side of the hall and as I stood up, they attacked and I vividly remember one guy's head bouncing along the stage leaving a trail of blood. It was all over in seconds and they were ushered from the building. But the management had other ideas and stopped the dance.

Then Mary told me that she was pregnant. How did I feel? How did she feel? We were in love and so it made sense that we should get married. Mary had told her mother whose first question was

"He is going to marry you?" Yes of course. She had given in her notice at the insurance company where she worked and been overloaded with gifts, which left me with the task of telling my parents.

I got in about ten that evening to find just my mother and brother at home. My mother couldn't contain her temper and I understood and kept quiet, turning to Mac she asked if he knew. He stood there open mouthed not knowing what to say after all he was my big brother! But how on earth could he have been in anyway responsible. She was so disappointed in me and as we'd been so close, and I felt bad because I'd let her down. In truth we were back to her relationship or non-relationship with neighbours, that they would talk about me, us and she hated that. I set out my strategy, getting married and going to live with Netta and Tom and then waited for Dad to arrive home but she insisted that I went to bed saying that she would tell him. Later I was woken by someone gently tapping my face. Dad was smiling at me "Alright?" he said. "Yes" I replied, and that was it.

The next day I was working on the Forshaw as part of my apprenticeship. This was away from the steel-works where slag would be tipped into the sea, and also coal and coke stored when I was told that someone wanted to see me, it was Dad. We talked about my plans for the future and he seemed satisfied particularly that I would continue with my apprenticeship and from then on things became easier to deal with. Tom was ill and was soon discovered to be suffering with bowel cancer and our marriage approached, he was in hospital recovering from a major operation. On the day of our marriage at the registry office in Park Place was Mum and Dad, Mac and Sally, Netta and her nephew Ronnie and Mrs Evans, someone Netta had worked for and who'd become a friend. We all returned to Danyrodyn and later that day Mary and me set off for our honey moon at Lavernock and a caravan Dad had bought. We couldn't see then that it was old and falling apart, we were free at last and in each other's arms as we planned our future together.

At work I was surprised by the number of people in the same situation. There were apprentices, some who'd got married and some who were still thinking about it. There was no embarrassment and certainly no shame involved. One foreman when finding out that I was married asked if I had a child. "No" I replied "But you've got your order in?" he said with a smile.

Living in Pentyrch was easy. We lived in a cul-de-sac of council houses where most of the tenants were original inhabitants of the village who took up residency when their previous homes had been demolished. Netta's next door neighbours were the same ones she'd had at Temperance Road, and those people across the road who I soon got to know were all smiles on our wedding day. Mary had arranged the house as she wanted though Netta was loathed to let us use the front room, the parlour that is as a living room, but whenever friends visited this was no problem. Tom came home from hospital with a colostomy and Mary became adept at changing his bags and when Jeremy arrived everyone was delighted, no one more so than my mother.

The bond mini car which had so often let me down worked perfectly when I took Mary and her carefully prepared bag to St David's hospital that night and as was the rule in those days, I had to leave her there where she stayed for the obligatory ten days. At what stage in your life do you think of your mortality.

I thought of it then as I walked up to the telephone box to phone my parents and then three years later when Sarah was born. 'Just enough time please, to see them grow up'. Mostyn and Peg lived across the road and at the time I didn't really know them but she was in St David's having her son who would grow up with Jeremy. Mostyn had a motor bike so I offered to take him at visiting time and he would turn to the left off the main corridor and I to the right until one night we both entered the wrong wards. I realised immediately what we had done and looked for Peg I walked across to her. "Hello" I said. "How are you tonight?" The woman sat up stiffly eying me as she defensively drew the sheet up to her chin. It wasn't Peg! It would have taken too long to explain so I quickly turned and left.

The winter of 63-64 was very cold but fortunately we were not as snow-bound as the previous year. Jeremy at almost three months of age suffered with a croup-like condition which our doctor, Dr Monger feared it could become pneumonia and advised us to keep him in an even temperature. The bedrooms were particularly cold and with no central heating and perhaps because of the altitude of Pentych it meant that condensation from our breath formed as ice on the inside of the window-pane, so the living room seemed the safest place. Mac enjoyed playing the cornet which he played in the St Albans' brass band for a while, then later playing the trumpet in a semi-professional dance band which during their interval our rock 'n' roll group would play. I played guitar and sang; Mac came out the dance band to play bass and as usual sing backing vocals with Lyndon. The drummer was Tubby Driscoll. The gig I remember vividly was at Wenvoe golf club and apart from rock 'n' roll songs we sang songs by the Beatles, Dave Clark Five, Johnnie Kidd all of which seemed to be getting a lot of air-play and when we finished our set the audience would not let us leave the stage, much to the annoyance of the band leader. I realised then that everyone liked what we did, and rock 'n 'roll and 'pop music' had crossed over to adults and was no longer just for teenagers, and it was thanks in the main to the Beatles. Someone approached me after the gig and even Dad who was transporting our gear, thinking he was our manager, but I just wanted to get home. Returning home, I walked quietly up the side alley to the back of the house and looking through the window, by the glow of the coal fire, was Mary and Jeremy and I resolved never to leave them like that again.

In nineteen sixty-four I bought a nineteen forty-six Austin 8 complete with an ant's nest in the glove compartment and which worked spasmodically. In the summer of that year, we went for a holiday to Cornwall. Glyn, Mary's uncle had always been a friend to Mary. There's a nice photo of him and Mary aged about four walking together hand in hand and it was he and his wife, another Mary who had arranged a cottage for us in Port Isaac. We packed our clothes in a trunk which had the initials MP, for Marion Peters stencilled on it and it lay on the back seat and on top of this was a carry-cot in which Jeremy lay. At one stage near Torrington when climbing a steep hill, the clutch began to slip so much that I was stationary. Mary got out and attempted to push the car and with only a little effort by her the car began to move. We enjoyed the holiday but since Glyn had lost his savings book on the way down, we provided the cash initially, and when Glyn was solvent again, he asked his Mary to settle things with Mary but somehow, we lost out which we could ill afford on an apprentice wage. Before leaving Mary telephoned her other auntie Margaret, Glyn's sister and explained the situation and her husband, Bob who was also an electrician was only too pleased to help us out. We met him at a pub just outside Bristol and he insisted that we stay the night with them and when Glyn and Mary arrived, they were also invited. From then on, Bob became a good friend but he also liked his beer and that night the three of us went to his local. Glyn who wasn't used to beer became more and more fascinated by a woman wearing a back-less dress and it was all I could do stop him touching it. It was late by the time we got back to the house to find Glyn's Mary had gone to bed in apparently a foul mood because we were late. Coupled with this a line prop had hit her while pegging out clothes and Margaret and Mary did their best not to laugh however it was hard to ignore the rumpus when poor Glyn went up.

I continued with my studies at Tech where Mary and me enjoyed the social life especially dances. Here I met Frank Hennessy who wanted to, and became a folk singer. I began to write songs and one friend, Robin Cullen who I met at Tech asked me to perform at a celebration in a public house at Llandough and not wishing to let him down I asked Lyndon to join me. It was going to be a long night and fearing that our make-shift Everly's and Beatles songs with just an acoustic guitar might not be enough we asked his mother, Dorothy to come along.

Dorothy was an accomplished pianist because Netta had spent a significant amount of money making it happen but it wasn't misspent and her aptitude for piano playing was incredible. It was said that there was always music emanating from their house at Temperance Road. She had travelled with an all-female accordion orchestra across the country and had only ceased when she had become pregnant. This was one of those events destined to dictate a way in life that might otherwise have been so different. She'd had Raymond a few years later and then Glenville when she was thirty-five but at forty, she'd kept her looks and more importantly was able play everything from the thirties to the present day without needing a musical score. As she got older, she could earn some extra money playing at old-people's homes or at the local pubs, extra to that which she made making bows at a local factory. Later on, in the sixties Albie divorced her claiming her infidelity and when I was asked by Netta to perhaps try to change his mind I discovered that he had every right. And when I spoke to a contemporary of hers some years later, she maintained that Dorothy was spoilt as a child rarely attending school, and it later seemed that she was vulnerable believing those men who paid attention to her.

The whole night was a success and a few years later when Rob and his wife turned up at the house and as was the tradition then or perhaps because of baby-sitting issues he and I went to the pub. There he told me that he'd met the love of his life and that he was going to divorce his wife and marry her, and it was pretty much settled. Back at the house Mary told me later that his wife had said that Rob had been somewhat distant but coming up to see us that night she was sure that things would turn out for the better!

I was nearing the end of my apprenticeship where during its course we'd spend six months in each department and by this time I'd given up my ambition of being an engineering draftsman and settled for a life 'on the tools'. Colin Phipps was the electrician at the melting shop where steel was heated in furnaces before being 'tapped' and run off into ladles. He cheekily ran a domestic electrical firm and surreptitiously had the telephone department of the works arrange a direct line to the work shop which he would use in his business. I worked for him in my spare time the money supplementing my apprentice wage and would often take over if a breakdown occurred in the melting shop. Me and the mate, who was supposed to just carry the tool bag but in reality, had a wealth of experience and was always worth listening to. Phippsy and me got on well but there was something about his personality that I was wary of. We went to his house-warming party with a friend and his wife who had once been Phipps' girlfriend and was amazed by the way he tried to seduce her under the nose of her husband, bearing in mind he'd just moved in with his new wife and child. Later in life I met him at an electrical wholesaler where he was returning Christmas lights, he'd failed to sell from a suit case door to door. Later again he made headlines locally after being arrested for running a brothel, it seemed that nothing mattered to him except making money. When I met Jane Buttle daughter of Lil, she told me how her husband had joined him in another business venture only to be left near bankruptcy.

The steel works always seemed an oppressive place to me and in many ways' claustrophobic. At about this time I rewired Auntie Flo's house in Porthamal Road, she'd recently re-married somewhat late in life, and her husband remarked poignantly one day, that steel works 'turned out steel and old men'. On occasions I had to climb the water tower where water was pumped up to a tank which by gravity fed parts of the works. It was by far the highest place and the Garth Mountain which was seven miles away almost looked within touching distance. I felt such an affinity to the place, hiraeth I suppose for the village and Mary. Once, when we were courting, I was travelling the two-mile hill to the village by bus and looking at the mountain through the window, there was the Garth and its three-thousand-year-old barrow outlined against a grey and foreboding sky and I had the sudden urge to climb it there and then. Mary was aghast at my suggestion but we were to climb it many times after that together and with our children. I began to be absorbed into the village.

Mary bought our groceries from the Twyn Shop run by her Uncle Rowland and his son would deliver them in a cardboard box. To begin with the box was marked Mary John, then some months later Mary John Thomas and eventually Mary Thomas.

In nineteen-sixty-five we moved to our own house across the road which had two bedrooms and was ideal for us, and the joy of having a place of our own was wonderful. We set about collecting furniture and were grateful for items donated by our families until we had everything we basically needed.

About this time, I met Dennis Treeby, his father-in-law had managed the rugby team I'd played for and Dennis' wife had been in Whitchurch school with us. His father was secretary of the musician's union in Cardiff, and Dennis was insistent that I met him and played him some of my songs. His father was most complementary but the atmosphere was strained and when a teenage girl came in, who was actually Dennis' daughter I understood why. Dennis had a wife and three children in Pentyrch. Stan Stennett, a gifted entertainer had been a neighbour of theirs in Cardiff but now lived on Rhiwbina Hill and Dennis took me there to meet him. He told me to go and see Pat Sherlock a music publisher at Mills music and generously telephoned him while we were there. From his phone conversation it seemed that they'd both played football for a charity showbiz eleven. A few weeks later Mike Evans, a friend from Rhiwbina who had visited a few times volunteered to drive us on the five-hour trip to London. The three of us set out early in the morning on the A40 road via Gloucester, Chelmsford and Oxford, and even though parts of the M4 had been built it was less confusing to stay on the old trunk road, and somewhere after High Wickham we looked down at London, and it's tallest building, the Post Office Tower. We found Denmark Street and Mills Music and were welcomed by Pat and sitting in his office and playing my guitar I sang him four songs. He seemed impressed and asked me to sing them again this time recording the songs and when we were leaving, he told me that he was confident that he could find artists to sing them.

Home, then to work the next day with the feeling that perhaps being a songwriter was not out of the question and that I was not destined to spend my life in the steelworks. About this time shift-work raised its ugly head when during the summer, electricians who worked shifts permanently took their holidays and those on a day shift, like me were obliged to cover for them for two weeks at a time. Mary found this particularly hard and I tried to do it as little as possible.

The steel works was at its worst during a night shift, repressive and inhuman and it's no wonder that surgeons struggle at times in the early hours. It's hot, sweaty and uncomfortable in overalls changing a broken-down motor on the roller tables. When we were apprentices, we were allocated three pairs of green overalls which distinguished us from the rest, one you currently wore, the second at the cleaners and the third in your locker. Many pranks were played such as smearing battery acid around the waist which at first was undetectable but over time holes would appear until eventually the trouser part would detach from the upper part. It wasn't unusual to see someone with ties made out of wire keeping both halves together. This could lead to a vendetta where when someone knew the culprit, they would carefully place a billy-can full of water in the perpetrators locker so that it leaned against the door and when the door was opened it would soak the opener. This became so personal that the one who placed the can would do the same in his own locker so the victim, seeking vengeance would get soaked a second time!

The passage-way beneath the rollers was the domain of the cats. The tom cats bearing scars like boxers who'd been in a fight. Independent, aloof and used to the scales dropping from the hot bars above – but don't touch them, they're wild. One of the mates took a kitten home once even though we'd warned him but after a week he'd brought it back.

But at least changing a motor ate-up time which otherwise might have been spent finding things to do, our prime role on a night shift was to be there in case of a breakdown. In every part of the works electricians had a workshop which was only accessible with a key and had a log book that told the following electrician what had or hadn't happened during the previous shift. Apart from our lockers it had a table and two benches and tea making facilities and it wasn't unusual on this particular shift to 'nod off' after supper but if the alarm blew, twice for an electrician you immediately left the workshop to solve the problem – the production manager 'breathing down your neck.' This was acceptable, more or less until a new works manager took it into his head to visit the plant in the early hours of the morning and, according to the Western Mail newspaper he'd found men in their pyjamas in sleeping bags! An exaggeration no doubt, but from then on, the regime was tightened and if your door was closed, and we had Yale locks, it could be construed that you were sleeping. The production manager on the rolling mill panicked when he saw us wandering about the mill grabbing me and asking "What's wrong?" Nothing!

With the demise of industry and the lack of apprenticeships I feel that many young people are missing out on the next stage of their learning. A rite of passage perhaps that is hard to substitute. In a steel works of some five thousand men, I met the good and the bad, the happy and the troubled and how to steer clear of those could be dangerous to know. Winston was forty and a bachelor who told me one day, holding back his tears how he'd lost his friend. His voice faltering as he described the night his friend had climbed out of their taxi in the pouring rain only to be hit and killed by a passing car. During our conversations I had mentioned Mary and when it became common knowledge that I 'had to get married' he approached me anxiously to ask "It is Mary. Isn't it?"

The war had been over for fifteen years but being young it could have been a lifetime away until you met people, survivors who were often loathed to tell of their experiences.

The group before I joined. Graham Parsonage, Mac, Steve Grey, on tea chest bass, Haydn Jones, John Downing and Clive Seddon on washboard.

The Rockets playing at Rhiwbina Fete complete with rockets sewn on to our red shirts courtesy of Mum.

Mum, Aunty Lyn, Uncle Em with Alun behind and first wife June.

Tea at Danyrodyn. Lynette, Tom, Lyndon
Netta and kids. (Alongside) Me, Mary
and Sarah. (Below) Bev, Mac and Mary.
(Alongside) Dad, Mum and Mary. (Below)
Bev, Sarah, me and Mum. (Alongside) Mary.

One man was deaf and always struggling with his hearing aids. He said that is hearing had been perfect until the day the tank he was controlling was hit by a German shell. Another had been at Dunkirk and always seemed to be happy though we suspected his happiness masked his experiences. "We were on the beach, pressed up against the dunes, trying to get as much cover from flying bullets as we could when a sailor rowed a boat in to the shore to take men off the beach. I was in charge of six men and we were given strict orders not to move until we had a signal. We watched as about fifty men ran to the boat and climbed in. The boat sank, and the sailor walked towards us cursing, waving his hands in disgust shouting 'you try to do someone a favour,' and all the while oblivious to bullets whizzing past him and what seemed like thunder and lightning going on all around."

Early in nineteen sixty-six and with no word from Pat Sherlock I took another trip to London, this was with Rob Cullen, Mary and Rob's wife, (before their marital difficulties) this time to Robins Music who had shown an interest and rather impetuously I took my songs from Pat, much against his wishes and left them at Robins when perhaps I should have left them with Pat.

In February Lyndon walked into the Junction Hotel in Taffs Well and struck up a conversation with some members of a band who were staying there. They were the Del 5 from Newcastle and had a list of gigs at working men's clubs in the valleys. He told them of my song writing and later that afternoon I went back with him where I played them some songs in the guitarists room. He liked one in particular and then dragged a large Grundig tape recorder from under his bed and recorded the song. Kim who fronted the band was sweet and was managed by club owner Ray Grehan, she proved to be an accomplished performer when we saw them a few nights later. The rest of the band, all boys were characters and Good Company. As I had no phone, I would often give out Dad's telephone number when asked and at the beginning of March he came up to tell me that someone from the Noel Gay agency was trying to get in touch. When I called him back, he wanted to know if the song was free and when I said it was, he told me he would be down the following day to meet me. I met him at Cardiff Central station and during the evening and after being plied with drinks he presented me with a contract explaining the benefits of having Ray as a manager and that many writers had managers working for them. After I'd signed the contract, he excitedly told me that the song Don't Take Your Lovin' Away had been recorded by Kim and that everyone was thrilled with the outcome and it had been accepted for release on the Decca label under the name Kim Davis. It was to be released that month to coincide with a support slot the band had secured on the Roy Orbison/Walker Brothers tour starting that month, but sadly even though they sang it every night and announced it as their latest record all their exposure had been lost when it wasn't available in the shops until June! When I received a copy through the post I treasured it, the Thomas beneath the title meant at least, in part I was a songwriter. It had plenty of plays on Radio Luxemburg where it was one DJ's record of the week and it was something of a thrill to walk into Dorothy's one evening to hear it being played on Luxemburg. It also had plays on the BBC's Light Programme this was before Radio One of course.

Back in April Kim and the band made contact before they arrived in Cardiff to invite us down but in the meantime, I had called at the home of the manager of the Capital who lived in Rhiwbina and whose daughter had been in junior school with me so Mary and me were given passes.

At this point we were settled in our own council house Jeremy was two and a half years old and Sarah was due to be born in the November. I had a secure job and often did jobs locally to earn extra money as an electrician. We intended therefore, to only watch the first show which started at 6.15pm as I was due to work a night-shift at 10.00pm.

We arrived at the Capital and watched the support acts including Kim from the back of the theatre then some of the band members were at our side to take us back-stage. We watched Roy Orbison from the aisle but unfortunately the young audience were not very appreciative but when the Walker Brothers stepped on stage the noise was deafening and they could hardly be heard over the screams. We left the theatre after the first show and had an enjoyable time in a bar listening to stories and anecdotes from the band members. Back at the theatre Mike, the drummer introduced us to Roy who was charming and modest. His father was sitting alongside him and another guy and they were all likeable Texans. I didn't realise then but the 'other guy' was singing harmony with Roy 'off-stage' and his name was Bill Dees who had co-written Pretty Woman and It's Over and went on to write for many country artistes.

Mike told us that Roy and the others travelled on the bus with them while the Walker Brothers travelled in a limousine and at a road side café when someone discovered that Roy was on the bus, he was happy to sign autographs. There was a window in this large dressing room where it seemed all the acts or perhaps all the male members congregated and if the window was opened it looked down on an alley which was crammed with teenage girls. When anyone looked out there was a loud scream from below which was a continual source of amusement as someone would say "I'll just give my ego a boost" before opening the window.

We watched the second show from the wings and Kim announced me by name as writer of the song and after failing to pronounce Pentyrch said that I was from near Taffs Well. This was met with a cheer from the now more mature audience and the band looked across and gave me the thumbs-up, Lulu was then at my side saying 'I love this song, you must write one for me' which was nice and perhaps made me feel that this could be my life.

I still felt it my duty to fulfil my obligations to do the night-shift, someone was relying on me to turn up but rationalising it the steel works would still operate without me. When I mentioned it in the bar, the fact that I was thinking of going into work was met with disbelief by the band, and they soon talked me out of it, much to Mary's delight.

On the 28th of October this year Granch died and was later buried at Aberfan cemetery alongside his wife and daughter, truly the end of an era for the house in Elm Street where my mother, her brother and sisters were born and bred and was now empty. The Aberfan disaster had happened a few weeks before and following the hearse, one could see the impact it had had on the faces of the people who looked pale and drawn, the men lifting their hats as we passed. A few months later in nineteen sixty-seven we travelled the same route when we buried Auntie Dilys and I sat next to a heartbroken John Evans. Heartache is what you get for loving.

At the end of November Sarah was born and we couldn't have been happier. For some unknown reason we both thought we would have another boy but having her was an unexpected delight and among the cards we received celebrating her birth was one from my mother saying 'thanks for a little girl'. The fact that the record didn't 'hit' seemed immaterial. The guitarist stated that it was too loud for the radio, but some had played it and, in any event, there would always be other songs.

In nineteen sixty-seven life became harder particularly for Mary when I was to work three shifts, me, a mate and an apprentice covering the Morgan Mill.

When I was in-between cars, I found myself walking the two-mile hill from Pentyrch to Taffs Well at five in the morning to catch the Dowlais to Cardiff bus. Iron making had started in Dowlais, Merthyr where all the ingredients were at hand but eventually with the making of steel, a purer ore was needed and this came into the docks at Cardiff, so another steel works was built there. Many men moved to Cardiff from Merthyr bringing their culture and language with them and many Welsh chapels sprung up in Splott in the early nine-teen hundreds. There was Ainon, Walter Road, Bethlehem in Eyre Street, and Jerusalem in Manon Street where I played banjo aged fourteen with Cwmni Wenallt. The bus that came through Taffs Well was something of a left-over for those wanting to remain in Merthyr and was supplied by the company.

Walking down the hill at five o clock in complete darkness I could see what I assumed was an animal in front of me and I approached it cautiously only to find that the four legs belonged to two men, Selwyn and Bill. They worked as bricklayers lining the furnaces after the molten iron had been taken out so the job by its very nature was hot and dusty. When I had a car on the road, I'd bring them home but their first port of call after finishing at 10.00pm was a pub to replenish the liquid they'd lost during their shift. Bearing in mind that closing time was 10.30pm and by the time we arrived it was well after 10.00pm we had fifteen minutes to drink three pints of beer! I drove home perfectly but when I got in and opened my mouth to speak, I was 'pissed', so I determined not to keep up with them ever again. Selwyn was a quiet and intelligent man who had discovered that his wife was having an affair with a neighbour. This being just one of the many hazards linked to shift work, particularly night shifts. Whether he found them together or not I don't remember but when he discovered the deception, he certainly took it out on the man, so that everyone was aware of the situation and his wife and the man left the village. When I met him later, he told me that one of his two daughters who had both chosen to stay with him had just married a school friend.

Towards the end of sixty-seven I'd managed to get back on day shifts and both Mary and me were happy. The work I was doing suited me that of wiring control panels and installing them and when I left one of the engineers had said to a friend of mine that 'they shouldn't have let me go' which was nice.

Who were they? At this time, I met Gwen Goodliffe's partner, she who went to art classes with Mum. I had never really spoken to him and he was employed by a contracting company to oversee an installation. He told me that he missed the sound of music emanating from number 43 Porhamal Road when he passed the house taking his dog down to Hill Snook Park. Also, in conversation I found that he and Gwen were not married but they'd been happy together for many years which made me reappraise Selwyn's situation. At this time, I was allocated a new electricians' mate and to my surprise it was Jack Yates. Jack had been manager of the Monico cinema, Rhiwbina where Mary and me spent many a night. He would greet people in the foyer, wearing his dinner suit and was the emblem of the cinema and here he was in his overalls, and in his middle to late fifties. He was quite philosophical about his change in life and being new to industry in general was eager to learn, though I did wonder about him scaling ladders with a tool bag and I wasn't the only one. On route to a job, we met someone wearing a suit and a white safety helmet which marked him out as management and he immediately recognised Jack. His name was Keen and was a descendent of one of the original founders of the steel works. "Good heavens Jack. What are you doing here?" And when Jack told him he said. "Come and see me I'm sure we can find something else". But Jack said he was happy and when I left, he was still an electrician's mate. It turned out that Jack was a freemason and was also steward of his lodge and as I got to know him, and him me, we had many discussions. He also asked me to do some electrical work at a house he was painting for the widow of a freemason and from then on, we did many jobs together, 'fiddles' because they weren't declared. The fact that he'd sat next to the Duke of Edinburg at his lodge didn't interest me but when he said if anything happened to me, they would make sure that my children would go to good schools and that was a fact worth thinking about. Don't worry about the cost he said, one of these (fiddles) would cover it and I was still thinking about it when I left in nineteen sixty-eight. The reason for me leaving, again shift work!

I was expected to work shift relief but I 'ducked and dived' and avoided it until I was cornered and then given an ultimatum. 'Even though you don't like it and your wife doesn't like it it's in your contract you must work it or else!' In my naivety I thought the management were to blame but it wasn't them, it was the union. The convener, the guy who took my subscriptions every month a guy I knew but had said nothing to me. A few nights later when we visited Mum and Dad, Dad who was a buyer for the company, took me into the front room. To my surprise he knew everything about my situation and told me of the union's involvement, and that the chief engineer was in the process of sorting it out, all I had to do was shift relief for two weeks, just three night shifts? I said no.

John Curran Engineering had won a contract to make run-up stands, this was a three roomed unit which went on the runway when an aircraft engine was tested and the main room was much like that of a cock-pit. The contract was for ten of these, and I secured a job there, and shortly after two of my friends from the steel works followed.

Sarah frightened us when she contacted gastroenteritis and had to be hospitalised, and at about eight months old this was hard for all of us to deal with. She was so upset when we left her that after two days, I signed her out. Dr Monger was very supportive and called every day until she was well.

He was a doctor in the old tradition and loved the area and had been inside the mine-pits and taken photographs of the huge caverns and lakes inside the lesser Garth. He wanted to open them and make them safe so that tourists could visit but failed to gain the interest of those who could make it another Wookey Hole. He was a painter and took a great deal of interest in the few paintings by my mother that hung on our walls and he had also written a book about his formative years. One day John Thomas, then living in Gwaelody Garth had sat in the waiting room at the doctor's house in Taffs Well until it was his turn to see him. Dr Monger who knew him by reputation could not find notes of any previous visit. John explained that he wasn't ill and that after reading his book he'd felt he had to come along and tell him how much he'd enjoyed it! His grandson is Chris Monger who directed the film An Englishman Who Went Up A Hill.... credited Dr Ivor Monger for the story about the Garth Mountain.

But when he took part in a radio program promoting the film Don Llewellyn, Chaiman of our local history society took him to task stating that the tumult was a three-thousand-year-old burial mound! To this Chris replied "Well at least we can say that it is man-made!"

I was still writing songs and at the end of sixty-seven or the beginning of sixty-eight I wrote There's Something About Suburbia. Though Pentyrch was a village rather than a suburb the song was more about the feeling I had when leaving the steelworks after a shift and heading home to Mary and the family and also her support and comfort when things didn't work out in 'the city'. Using Dad's trusty Philips, I sang the melody and played the guitar then while playing this back I sang again and played piano recording both on a second borrowed, tape-recorder. I had often bought the Record Mirror and enjoyed the column written by Tony Hall, a one-time Luxembourg DJ and presenter of the TV show Oh Boy which Mac and me had watched avidly and when he said that he was leaving the magazine to set up a pop music company I decided to send him the song. He came back saying he liked the it and invited me up to London so, Mary and me met him at his flat cum-office in Carnaby Street. The girls in the office wore mini, miniskirts and Mary felt a tad old fashioned and when we got back to Pentyrch she wore her dresses in that same style though Pentyrch wasn't perhaps ready yet to move with the times.

As we talked it transpired that he knew and liked Don't Take Your Lovin' Away and was partly responsible for its release on the Decca label. We also met Paul Korder who was going to produce the song which was to be sung by Tim Andrews. We then visited the publishers, Essex Music where Tony asked me to record the song again explaining that the tape of my original recording was now 'the worse for wear'. I had a habit of using the same tape over and over and then by the time they had played it several times the quarter inch tape resembled a piece of string! I sat at the piano with a microphone in front of me and within minutes of me finishing the song Tony came out of an adjoining room with an acetate record of the song. It was equipment I could only dream of.

When I heard the finished recording a month or so later, I was disappointed that they'd altered the structure of the song which was something Tony had particularly liked, that is the way the song built. My version has verse1, verse2, bridge, chorus, instrumental and repeat chorus to finish. Their version had verse1, chorus, verse2, chorus instrumental then a Chorus to finish. I remember Tony saying that the song would make me a lot of money but it wasn't to be.

As the year progressed, they had doubts about the popularity of the song saying that teenagers would rather be leaving suburbia for the city rather than going home to it and perhaps they were right. In May of that year Suburbia was released as a B side, the A side being a song entitled Your Tea Is Too Strong written by Tim and Paul but as it sometimes happens the DJ's preferred to play 'Suburbia' so that most of the royalties I received were generated from radio 'air play' and eventually it was termed 'a turn-table hit'. Indeed, Howard told me later that while in college he'd seduced an American student on the back of knowing the writer. Aunty Lyn (Eluned) wanted a copy and she and my mother went into Cardiff and James Howells where the ladies working there excitedly told them that they'd just missed the writer of the song. This puzzled my mother who knew that I'd changed jobs and was hardly likely to leave work during the day. It was Mac, posing as me in, retrospect I should have used him more he would have made a great manager.

The record didn't sell that well but one day one of the electricians who had joined me at John Curran told me that it was in the top thirty and that he'd heard it stated on the radio! It was actually Tony Blackburn's Fun Thirty! It made me a thousand pounds in royalties, which was quite a lot then but apart from buying a four-track tape recorder the rest just disappeared no doubt on things for the home and family. Tony suggested firstly that I should think about coming up to London to 'hang out' with writers and producers but for how long, and with no guaranties, and leaving Mary it was out of the question. He then suggested that I meet Kingsley in Monmouth who had a small studio in a potato loft on their farm but that he and his brother Charles had big plans for Rockfield. They'd recorded a song called River to Another Day by Love Sculpture featuring Dave Edmunds which Tony had tried to promote but the record, like Suburbia hadn't been successful.

In nineteen sixty-nine Mum and Dad moved from Porthamal Road to Heol Ifor in Whitchurch. It was to a bungalow which my mother had always wanted and my father was happy enough to indulge her though perhaps he didn't realise the plans Mary and my mother had for the new place. My father lived his life with the attitude that if it's 'not broke why fix it' and though he thought nothing of buying a fridge, television or a stereo radiogram when it came to furnishings, he definitely had a blind spot. Mary was horrified one day to find my mother weaving wool into a part of the carpet which had become threadbare and from then on, they both decided that things were going to be different, and they were. At Netta's house she looked after the purse strings and Tom duly gave her his wages which together with her own meant that she managed the home and any household bills. When we were courting, I remember Mary taking pity on him one day and altering his pay slip so that he had a little bit more for tobacco and beer. They had met in Nanymoel where Netta had been in service and they later returned to her home village. Prior to this he had served in the army during the First World War and had been injured at Ypes for which he received a small pension for a while. He had been a collier and a quarry worker at Creigiau and was indeed a character, playing the piano in a unique style he could also tap-dance in an original way. A small man he had sparred with a Cuthbert Taylor who had been sent to the quarry to build up his muscles and managed to stay out of his way until the break was over. When the bus turned over on the Creigiau Road they searched for him in vain because he had run home to Netta who he trusted to see to his injuries, and after an accident in the quarry where 'Cock Robin' (his nickname) was seriously injured, he asked Tom to roll a him a cigarette before he died. Then when a rock crushed Tom's finger, the Infirmary in Cardiff wanted to amputate but Netta sent Mary into the garden to collect snails with which she made a bread poultice. Netta's house was used as a surgery for Dr Thomas from Morganstown, the parlour that is, and a cupboard housed some of his equipment. Tom could remember being called in to hold somebody down while Dr Tom performed a circumcision. Ouch! He also favoured the use of the poultice and some weeks later just the top joint of Tom's finger fell into the bowl, but not before he'd spent many a night walking the village in an attempt to distract him from the pain, but it healed and he was still able to play the piano.

Many other things happened during this year. Firstly, we moved across the road to number 19 Heol Danyrodyn which was a three-bedroomed house. The local council stipulated that if you had two children of opposite sex, they needed to have their own bedrooms, and even though we had plenty of time to make a decision when the house became vacant, we took it. The house also had the added bonus of having a telephone.

Howard, after leaving college had started teaching at Canton High and soon after a student had arrived and they had become friends. Claude was from Bordeaux and was still learning English and Howard couldn't resist having fun with her, and because he was still living at home and she was 'in digs' they found it necessary to find somewhere to be together on weekends. On one such trip he told her it was polite to say 'fuck off 'to the conductor when he gave her their tickets. The man looked astonished at her while Howard gazed out of the window. Mary could drive the mini I had expertly, but had never taken a test and one evening we decided to take Claude home and because Howard and me had had a drink Mary drove while I was her slightly intoxicated 'competent driver'. I was chatting to them when Mary nudged me "What's this?" She asked. It was the first mini roundabout I'd ever seen but being late at night and with nobody around she negotiated it without a problem. In this year Claude and Howard were married much to the disappointment of his mother as Claude was expecting Isobel, and after briefly living in 'rooms' at the Philog they settled for a while in a house opposite his mother in Waun Treoda Road.

Music wise I recorded some songs at Sharland's studio in Cathays with Lyndon, Malc and Roy Smith, Mary's cousin that is on the John's side, playing drums. Sharland rushed out of the control room to tell me that I was playing the piano too loud? It's a percussion instrument I told him! And the song Sadie'll Have a Goodnight Tonight got used and recorded in different guises later on. One version was a translation called Ceri (am gael noson mor fawr) used at a later date in the Can I Gymru competition. During this year a woman turned up at the house from Gwent with some lyrics. When Suburbia came out articles appeared in the local press one giving out my address, and she had heard of the very first Song for Wales competition (Can I Gymru), which was to be run by BBC Wales and her words suited it very well. It was eventually won by Margaret Williams with a song in Welsh called Y Cwilt Cymraeg. The rules stated however, that the song had to be presented as a musical manuscript and luckily cousin Alun Francis sat alongside me at the piano and jotted the notation down. The song aired on the television but didn't live up to our expectations.

We met Kingsley and his wife who were easy to get on with. Unfortunately, they had recently lost a five-year-old daughter from viral pneumonia which had happened to cousin Marianne Glenda's daughter Leslie, a few months earlier and our hearts went out to them. During our conversation we agreed that I should find a young pop group who he would record, using my songs and he would produce them and I would become their personal manager.

Cousin Gwyn Francis (Niblo) loved his rock 'n' roll and was well known in Merthyr for his Little Richard style piano playing and he told me of a local band named Chapter Five who were a 'teeny bop' band with a male and female vocalist who could harmonise well together, and looked almost like a young Sonny and Cher. The band consisted of drums, bass, organ and guitar played by Dai Shell. Kingsley also liked them and immediately drew up some contracts for them to sign which I remember thinking was perhaps a little too soon and which proved to be the case. The parents of some of the band members were understandably worried about careers and apprenticeships and the situation wasn't helped by the enthusiastic Dai, who only wanted to be a musician and quickly gave up his day job. I tried to reassure the parents that nothing would happen until the songs had been recorded and the finished product appraised but to no avail and when I was contacted by an agency about the band playing in Germany, I began to feel uncomfortable about the responsibilities of management. Consequently, the bass player and drummer were replaced but the biggest loss was the male lead singer. We went ahead with a new vocalist but he had neither the voice or the image and so the original sound had gone.

In nineteen seventy I took the recordings up to Tony Hall and we played them at Essex Music to the then A and R man Graham Churchill but even I felt embarrassed as we sat and listened to the songs. Why didn't I sing myself I thought later?

I had left the engineering company when the units that we were wiring had come to an end, and after a brief spell working for contractors on the Heath Hospital site, I obtained a job with Cardiff Electrical Repairs. This suited me because I was employed to find the fault when motors began to malfunction in industry, and also to work on small installation jobs for a firm who were essentially motor rewind specialists.

In nineteen seventy Mac and Bev were married which turned out to be a long Catholic wedding which none of us were expecting not having been to one before. John (Tubby) Driscoll also a catholic was chosen as best man much to the disappointment of my parents. When some two years later I was best man to Vaughan on a sunny afternoon in the garden of the Kings Arms and delivered my carefully worked out speech Mac, who had driven Lorna to the church in his ribboned Jaguar, had enthused about my speech to my mother. She couldn't resist saying that maybe he'd picked the wrong best man. Dad made sure that all my uncles and cousins were there from Abercanaid and Troedyrhiw.

In this year I was surprised when Gus Saunders knocked on the door, I'd seen him occasionally because he and Howard had met in the grammar school and of course both knew me. When I asked how he'd found me he said he'd called in the pub, the Lewis Arms and said "Rod Thomas?" And someone had immediately directed him. It was still a small village.

He had with him the brother of another friend of ours from Rhiwbina Junior and left me with him while he disappeared with Mary. Martin Lewis was the drummer in a band and they wanted an original song that they could record as a demo. The band was Dormouse with Leighton and Brian John from Llanhari.

Eventually I met them and gave them a song called Fragile and shortly after I took them up to Rockfield to record it. Kingsley wasn't sure about it and neither was I as we had tried other songs with Chapter Five which hadn't worked.

Imagine my surprise when someone firstly phoned Mary from Major Minor records and later I received a publishing contract from Chapel Music. Major Minor had Mony Mony by Tommy James in the charts as well as the risqué Je t'ame. A few weeks went by and when I enquired Martin, instead of grabbing Major Minor's offer, had said that he thought he'd try some other companies first and left!! And so, the deal went cold!

The house at Danyrodyn had a long back garden with a natural bank at the end and many people who visited enjoyed shooting my air-rifle, complete with sights at targets positioned on the bank, Mac and Howard particularly.

I continued to work for Cardiff Electrical and found because I was out and about, I could pinch an hour here and there to call into the house, and after such a visit on my way to a factory on the

Treforest Estate I had a car accident on the narrow Williford Road. I broke my finger and kneecap and because of stitches in the gash, for two or three weeks my leg was in a cradle-type cast to begin with and later, a complete cast when I could use crutches.

Mary worked in the local Pegler's Stores and she enjoyed the company and the customers. Before we were married, she had worked at the post office until Aunty Doris had insisted that she take a civil service examination after which she took a job at the Wales Finance Office in Westgate Street before eventually moving on. At the shop she was happy and it was convenient for Jeremy who was in the village school and Sarah who had started at the Welsh school at Gwaelod y Garth. This was born out of an awareness that the language of my father and generations before him and one half of my mother's was in danger of dying and from nineteen sixty-six when Gwynfor Evans was elected as the first Plaid Cymru MP to enter parliament there was a general realisation by many that things could change. When Jeremy began school, the opportunity wasn't there but things were different for Sarah, even though she had to travel by mini-bus she settled well and had no trouble picking up the language, to the delight of my father. In nineteen seventy-one I saw the Triban on the television programme Disc a Dawn which was a live programme similar to Top of the Pops and they struck me as being as being very professional in their approach, with lovely three-part harmonies. The band consisted of Bob Richards, Caryl Owen and Jill Jenkins and since I'd been experimenting with my four-track tape recorder where I could layer my voice and instruments, I contacted Bob who immediately came up with his wife. We became friends for many years and he became a good sounding board. He firstly suggested that I should send a tape to Ruth Price who was producing Disc a Dawn and when I mentioned that I thought my Welsh wasn't good enough he was happy to admit that he didn't speak Welsh at all.

I sent a song to Ruth and when she called me it transpired that she knew my father because after newly arriving in Cardiff she had joined Cwmni Wenallt for a while. She was happy to get the song translated ready to be performed on the programme. "Bring your group in" she said, but there was no group, just me.

Soon after I received a Welsh lyric for my song Where Did You Go Last Night (I Ble Es Ti) with Lyndon the obvious choice to join me and over the next four years we were lucky enough to perform regularly on the show. Bob had a mobile home at Culverhouse Cross and I remember asking what 'birth' it was only to be corrected, it having two bedrooms! In truth it was like a bungalow and well laid out. One night at Bob's we were there having a drink with Max Boyce and his wife when the police turned up, but Max had them in 'stiches'. "I'm going about eleven. You've got a fast car, have you? You'll need it to keep up with me!"

Our first appearance on the show was televised from an old chapel at Broadway in the Splott area, where podiums were situated in the two corners of the chapel and once you had sung your song, you stepped down and were quickly replaced by the next performer while the camera switched to the person presenting the show. This could be among others Mici Plwm, Dewi Pws or Hywel

Gwynfryn who had translated the song. It was nice to get a note from Meredyth Evans who was head of light entertainment complimenting us on our performance. I had met him in nineteen sixty-nine when Gus' father had spoken to him about me but during our friendly conversation, he couldn't see any openings for Anglo Welsh songs. Dafydd Iwan was of the same opinion when we chatted during one Disc a Dawn show when he felt that if we were to have a Welsh language channel then BBC Wales and HTV would be able to accommodate Anglo Welsh talent, but that didn't happen.

In the summer of that year, I'd written Timothy Jones. When I was in the steel works, I remember one guy who had a shop run by his wife and he remarked on the women who'd buy a packet of crisps for 'Johnny's' tea because she was 'off to play bingo', and so came the idea of 'latch-key' kids. I had gone up to Rockfield to record it with Leighton on guitar, Mac on bass, Clive Seddon on drums an me on piano and mellotron, but when I'd returned to put the vocals on it didn't seem to work. Fortunately, Dave Edmunds was wandering about the studio and when I asked him if he would record another drum track, he was happy to oblige. It took about three takes and on an unremarkable drum kit, dampened with a blanket he transformed the track. I sent the track around without much reaction when Bob suggested Jonathan King.

That year the Triban had recorded a song called Black Paper Roses with him which had been released on Decca and the group then had comprised of Eiri Thrasher later to be replaced by Jill. According to Bob it was Eiri's voice that Jonathan liked and she went on to do a number of projects with him.

Mary and me.

Mine from 'Timothy Jones' session, they said 'make it moody!'

Below from our EP cover Rod a Lyndon recordiad a label Dryw, 1974

Me and Dad outside Blue Seas in Porthcawl with Nathan and Ruth.
Me and Mary outside the Post office at Bryn.
Mary, Elizabeth, Anne and Howard at Bryn. Jeremy and Sarah at Bryn.
Pontypridd Gateway Club on stage at one of the Gateway Festivals.
Me and Howard at Pentre Ifan and a very young Elizabeth.

On Christmas Eve of that year Mary and me travelled by train up to Olympic Sound studios, Barns, and met Jonathan and an engineer in a vast but empty studio. During the day a thirty-piece orchestra had recorded the backing tracks for four A sides including Timothy Jones so with Mary in the control room, all I had to do was put the earphones on and record the vocals. As we were leaving a group of girls arrived to record Don't Let Him Touch You, they were called The Angelettes.

On the way back on the train two things stick out in my mind firstly Barry John was in deep conversation with a man and one couldn't help hearing the name George Best being mentioned. It later turned out that Barry was trying to get a manager who could take him on the same path as George, modelling suits and the like but it was not to be and the following year he retired. The other was that Bernadette Devlin who I admired greatly for her stance against the overpowering protestants in the north and who was a member of parliament for mid Ulster was obviously on her way back home. As they came down the corridor, I smiled at her and received the briefest of smiles back but the henchmen walking before and after her were not going to stop.

Back at home and into nineteen seventy-two I received a call from Robin Griffiths who had seen us on Disc a Dawn. Apart from his job as an actor, one of them being the puppet Blodwyn Tatws on Miri Mawr he also researched, looked out for singers who could be used on the programme. The song that I had in mind was Peter Pan (Pitar Pan) which I'd written a few years earlier.

Daughter Sarah was one of those children who had much difficulty in getting to sleep, and I had painted a picture of Peter Pan on the starry wallpaper in her bedroom which I had copied from one of Mary's knitting patterns. She surely had an imaginative mind which she could not switch off at bedtime and so I spent many a night singing her quietly to sleep and that's how the song arose.

"What about Fi yw Pitar Pan?" I suggested and from then on, the song was translated with Robin and we performed it on Miri Mawr. I had left Cardiff Electrical and was now self-employed which made it easier to record the inserts down at the HTV studios at Pontcanna, terrapin huts as I remember, in the afternoons. It's hard to talk about money and value then compared to now, suffice to say that we were paid double the amount we had received from BBC, so when Ruth called, I mentioned this and she did increase our fee from then on. When we performed Pitar Pan on Disc a Dawn my mother had cleverly 'piped' my denim jacket with yellow which complimented the blue denim perfectly. During the break and in the canteen one of the production workers admired it only to add "It's a pity we're in black and white today!" In those days BBC Cymru only had one colour television camera and that day Wales were playing at home so the game took precedent. Max who appeared on the same show was in a flap that day and as I tried to tune his guitar, he was frantically trying to alter his lyric to Hymns and Arias. He'd translated it into Welsh but the BBC hierarchy did not like the suggestion that urine had been put in the bottle, aka "We gave them that bottle which once held bitter ale!"

The news came through of a release date for Timothy Jones.

Jonathan King usually leased his productions to other labels and was so successful that one day when I opened the NME to look at the charts, the top twenty that is, I turned the page to see another chart this time with a number of titles in red. He had placed this advert containing in red all of his productions. He had given the track to Cube Records a new label born out of Fly Records and it was to be the first single on their label. By coincidence they were actually part of the Essex group and the guy that had heard the Chapter Five songs was still in charge of A & R, and apologised for passing on my original demo, I diplomatically pointed out that the company now had a Jonathan King production. I had met him when Mary and me stayed with the man in charge of publicity, Dave Reffell when apart from visiting the office he and the photographer suggested an early start when the mist was still heavy on the lake at St James' Park where the photos were taken. Jonathan got in touch to say that he wanted me to record the B side so it was a taxi ride over to a smaller studio where he was recording BJ Arnau. I complimented her on her voice and the song she'd sung in Oh Calcutta which I'd heard and she was pleased and very modest. When she had left Jonathan gave me a white record sleeve on which he'd scribbled 'I went down to the railroad and there he was Arthur Smith, he's a big man Arthur Smith'. I put the earphones on to hear a twelve-bar blues backing track and thought about what I would sing when he told me not to sing but to recite the words. So, I ad lib'd to stretch it out, then it was done taking all of five minutes. He'd heard that I had signed a contact with Cube for the next single and he thought that I should have waited before signing and I wished that I'd spoken to him before signing. Later that day we visited the Luxemburg studio where a DJ called Tony Mercer was recording a programme and met Gilbert O Sullivan and Johnny Nash and we chatted freely before we took turns to sit alongside Tony who asked us questions and then played the record. We'd all had to wait while Marc Bolan did his interview as he'd refused to do it with us in the room and there were a few wry smiles over his prima donna attitude. It also turned out that Jonathan was supposed to be there but he didn't like Tony Mercer and from then on, his relationship with Cube seemed to deteriorate which did not bode well for the launch of the record when they were depending on him for promotion. In the end unbeknown to them Jonathan was launching his own record label called UK Records and Timothy Jones by the unknown Rod Thomas disappeared without trace. Later that evening we went out for a meal courtesy of Dave Reffell. "I don't mean to put him down but you know he's gay?" he said. Mary dug me "There you are I told didn't I!" Then a lovely night, the first time under a 'continental quilt', a duvet that is and decided that it was a must have when we got home.

When we performed for Ruth Price, she suggested that I should write a song for Can I Gymru which was to take place that year, and since I already had songs written in English I got together with Robin and we chose two to translate. They were Ceri (Sadie) and a new song Cana Gan (Sing the Song) and we were surprised when we learnt that both songs had made the final. Lyndon and me were to sing Cana Gan on the program and Ceri was to be sung by Bob and Eiri Thrasher. We performed Cana Gan first at Pebble Mill which was newly built and because the London people were loathed to travel to Birmingham at the time was something of a 'white elephant'. We stayed overnight and enjoyed the experience meeting up with Frank Hennessy again and Meic Stephens who I'd heard was something of a loose cannon. Hearing girls scream I opened the dressing room door to see him running up the corridor naked. There were also two groups one from Sir Fon and the other Caernarfon who had found it easier to get to Pebble Mill than to travel to Cardiff! The competition took place a month later at the studios at Llandaf when all six songs were performed in front of an audience. The competition was won by a lovely folk ballad called Pan Ddaw'r Dydd by Geraint Jarmon and sung by his then wife, Heather Jones. Ceri seemed to be a hit with the audience however because it was almost 'vaudeville' with a trad jazz feel complete with Bob wearing a straw boater. At the end of the night, I talked to Huw Jones who thought that my songs were 'to camp' for Can I Gymru. I took this on board and remembered it for the next time.

Disc a Dawn was transmitted live on a Saturday evening on BBC Wales but on the following Wednesday a recording of the show went out at lunch time on BBC One. Benny Litchfield who was musical director for BBC Wales alerted me to this saying that if my songs were published, I would receive performance royalties for my songs which were only a few pounds from BBC Wales but considerably more from BBC One. So it was that Benny and his Land Of Song Music, who published some ten titles for which he collected the royalties and duly paid me my share. This also happened with HTV though on one English language programme with actors Jack Walters and Elen Roger Jones I received payment for writing the songs as a commission. Benny lived at St Fagans with his lovely wife Molly who was in charge of wardrobe and later they moved to Mallorca.

When Jeremy was ten years old Vaughan Williams became his teacher at Pentyrch Junior School. At the time he was living in a caravan which was so poorly insulated that he swore the warmth from his Labrador Sara, kept him alive through the long winter nights. Sara was somewhat unpredictable and could sometimes wreck the caravan if left alone during the day so, Vaughan decided to bring her to school leaving her in the car where he could make frequent visits with food and water. One day she appeared alongside him in the classroom after eating her way out of his soft-topped sports car.

When I met him, Jeremy was playing a chubby villain in the musical Vaughan was staging along with a thinner boy who was his side-kick. Sitting in the audience before the show started, I was reading the New Musical Express while the father of the thin boy sat alongside me reading the Financial Times! Vaughan told me that he wanted to form a pop group using some children from the youth club he'd started but they needed a drummer and so I volunteered Jeremy. Jeremy had shown some talent using drum sticks that someone had left at the house and for Christmas seventy-two we'd bought him a drum kit. At first, he struggled to reach the bass drum and high-hat peddles but soon mastered them and could easily play along with me on guitar. Vaughan was speechless when we turned up at the rugby club for a rehearsal with a real drum kit, he was expecting some sort of a toy kit he told me later. He was equally amazed at Jeremy's expertise. By now I knew Peter Elias Jones who produced Miri Mawr and he was open to them auditioning and after they had learnt I Ble'r Es Ti they were ready to perform it. During the rehearsal Dewi Pws turned up alongside me and said "That drummer's good.

Who is he?" It gave me great pleasure to say that he was my son. So, in nineteen seventy-three they made their appearance, unfortunately, a video of this appearance doesn't exist, according to Don Llewellyn who was working there said many things were lost in a fire and we only have some photos which brother Mac took from the television. While there I met Phil Jones again from Porthamal Road who was editing some films to enable the inclusion of adverts. His grandfather was the author Jack Jones and his father had tried but failed as an actor and no doubt these credentials had helped him secure a job there.

Vaughan and me became firm friends and had many discussions over a glass of whiskey both at the caravan where Lorna now lived or at our house in Danyrodyn. They decided that I should become a teacher but as I explained I would have little patience with primary school children and no patience with teenagers who didn't want to learn. Also, he was a committed Christian and me being an atheist there were many differences of opinion. He called in one day when Howard was visiting and I was making a particular point about something, probably a book I'd read, since Howard was into literature and to which Howard graciously remarked that those were the feelings of academics. When I introduced them Vaughan who had gone to St. Luke's teachers training college wanted to know where Howard had gone to university and he replied Cardiff and after more interrogation Howard then said Oxford to which Vaughan was suitably impressed. It's strange how qualifications mean so much to some people. Someone once said that 'qualifications mean limitations.'

Together with Mary and Lorna we tried to learn ballroom dancing at Sibyl Marks which we enjoyed for a while and when we attended one of their rehearsals for a coming TV performance on Come Dancing, we met Gus once again. His wife was part of the team and when I introduced Vaughan there was some banter, some rivalry between Loughborough where Gus had gone, and St Luke's where Vaughan had gone after Millfield. I didn't pay much attention as to how he had found himself in Pentyrch because it was music which seemed to connect us and I knew nothing of his life before he had arrived in the village but gradually his story was revealed. He had been at Barry Grammar school when his talent as a rugby player was noticed and he was offered a scholarship at Millfield. When his widowed mother asked the headmaster how much it would cost, he answered "Whatever you can afford." He played outside-half to Gareth Edwards and the Millfield school team was very successful with many write-ups in the press praising his abilities. He played regularly for Wales Youth keeping Barry John out of the team and next went to St Luke's where he suffered some concussion in successive matches and seemed to lose his love for the game. At Pentyrch however, his interest had been rekindled and he had become the hero of many a cup competition until he had eventually 'hung up his boots'. He still had his competitive nature though, and when we thought that a game of tennis might be an interesting diversion, we found that none of us were in his league.

We continued with Disc a Dawn which the following year became Gwerin 74, and though we did some shows from Llandaf the show also went 'on the road' to places like Craig y Nos, Theatre Felin Fach and Theatre y Werin.

Mary was working at E C Cases when another girl in the office said "Did you see Lyndon Jones on the television last night. He's done well for himself!" I asked her if she had mentioned that the other guy was me, her husband, but no she was far too modest for that.

When Can I Gymru was advertised for this year and bearing in mind the words of Huw Jones I set about writing something that would be more appropriate? I thought about the struggles Wales had had through the centuries and wrote my verses beginning 'Did your forefather fight with Llewellyn? Did your forefather ride with Rebecca? Did your forefather bleed in a coal seam 'ac ati'. Robin did a great job on the translation and I was pleased with the demo. I then wrote another song with a lighter feel which I thought might be too radical, the first line being 'there's no God that I can see but my eyes are watching me'. Once again, to our surprise both songs I Gael Cymru'n Gymru Rydd (To Make Wales Free) and Fy Nghydwybod I (My Conscience) made the final.

Iris Williams was chosen to sing all the songs and would sing two songs on each weekly show before singing all six songs on the night of the competition. At Theatr y Werin in Aberystwyth, Lyndon and me were appearing on the same show as Iris and we were watching the rehearsals when she came to talk to us. Lynette, Lyndons wife is of mixed race and was born and brought up in Rhydfelin but her background was never really talked about only that we knew her mother but her father wasn't around. On their wedding day it was Mary who had stepped in when a question from the registrar left an awkward silence. So, Iris, being Iris wanted to know where she was from and did she know her father then jokingly finished with perhaps they had the same father, and that maybe he had a bicycle. Perhaps this was the way Iris dealt with who she was at a time when there didn't seem to be too many people of mixed race around.

The final took place at the studios in Llandaf and it was nice to have my father and mother in the audience and as well as Mary, Marged who had visited us many times with Robin. Marged Esli is an actor with a lovely personality and she and Mary always got on well together but strangely, to us that is, she and Robin were only good friends. Well, Cael Cymru Rydd came first and Fy Nghydwybod I second and we were delighted, and after much fuss and photographs and a night of praise and drinks at the BBC Club we arranged a meal at Rabaiotti's in Penarth the following Saturday when the four of us went out to celebrate.

Iris and the song then went to Ireland to take part in the Pan Celtic competition where songs from Ireland, Scotland, The Isle of Man, Cornwall and Brittany took part, and before going Rhydderch Jones, the producer asked me for the English words which of course I had to hand and which were given to the judges. The group Y Diliau had provided excellent vocal backing for the song and had travelled to Ireland with Iris and when the competition ended and Cael Cymru'n Gymru Rydd had won, Gaynor, one of Y Diliau telephoned her husband and asked him to let me know of the success. There was some altercation with the prize money but things were soon sorted and later that year Sain released an EP Record by Iris containing both songs.

In August, Vaughan and Lorna were married and he stayed the night before with us at Danyrodyn, then Mac drove us down to The Mission Church before picking up Lorna and bringing her and her father to the church. It was a lovely sunny day and the reception in the garden of The Kings Arms was perfect.

At the end of the year Lyndon and me recorded an EP at a recording studio in Swansea for the record label Dryw. At the studio we recorded Ceri, Paid a Phoeni and Cana Gan. The fourth song Joseph (Joseff) I had recorded in English at Draig Studios in Canton and it was about the life of the composer Joseph Parry. When we recorded the Welsh version, I asked Diliau to sing backing vocals which they did to great effect. Y Diliau consisted of Mileri Mair, who was a daughter of Gwynfor Evans, Gaynor Jones who had taught Sarah at Gwaelod y Garth school and had actually put a photo (a newspaper cutting) of me on the classroom wall, and Mair Robbins, another teacher who went through my Welsh lyrics with a red pen at a later date. The studio was used mainly by the group Sassafras with Dai Shell producing and who could also add a 'mean' guitar when asked, and one I had to replicate on the show Gwerin 74.

We started to play the working-men's clubs as a duo taking pot luck on the drummer as there was always an organist and a drummer in each club. Sometimes the drummer was 'tuned in' to the songs we played, an example being the Ex-servicemen's club in Taffs Well while in another the drummer, who had half of his ear missing had his trousers held up with a neck-tie.

In the meantime, Jeremy had come on 'leaps and bounds' with his playing and to me it seemed only logical that he should join us but Mary was unconvinced. She naturally worried about late nights and how it might affect his school work but eventually she agreed that we could try it out since our gigs were usually on a Friday and Saturday night, he could lie in if need be. He became the 'star' and I joked that whatever mistakes we might have made it didn't matter, because they were watching this eleven-year-old on the drums. One night when we must have played on a Sunday and were packing the equipment away Mary had said "Come on you've got school in the morning!" Then one inebriated club member who'd overheard said "School! What are you worrying about school when he can play drums like that!"

We continued to play the clubs of all shapes and sizes. Sassafras' manager also ran an entertainment agency from Seven Road and we sometimes worked for him. In Machen we played in a large wooden hut and when on stage the roof trusses were level with our heads, then two birds flew up and down the hall before perching on the beams. In the valleys some knew of us from Disc a Dawn so we were able to include Welsh language songs in the first spot. In the second spot we played rock 'n' roll when people wanted to dance. At this point, and during the first spot we went some way to being a cabaret act when Jeremy would leave the drums to sing and play a ukulele. Songs like The Ballad of Jesse James and Joe Brown's What a Crazy World We're living In.

In seventy-five we entered Can I Gymru with a folk song titled Dau Ceffyl Gwyn, (Two White Horses) which once again made the televised final.

This took place at Craig y Nos where I performed the song, this time without Lyndon, but we had an enjoyable time with Robin and Marged. The competition was not without controversy as the winning song was written by Dewi Pws. Dewi however, was working for the BBC at the time so at the last minute his song was disqualified. In the end the group Bran were the winners and our song moved up to second place.

I began to lose interest in club work when it became a chore. Lyndon didn't drive and it meant that he, or we had to find someone to take him to the venue. In our car we carried amps, a PA, guitars and a drum kit also Mary and Jeremy and sometimes Sarah, and it probably came to a head when we four were eating sandwiches on a New Year's Eve in a dressing room before having to go on for a second spot. Mary and me decided we'd had enough. We did perform after this when it was for some occasion or other and we knew we would enjoy the gig often playing for free. When a cook was retiring from E C Cases a leaving celebration was put on in the local club and during our performance, we sang Wait till The Sun Shines Nellie, that was her name, to which I written new, applicable words and we delivered it as a Barbour shop four, only we were three with Jeremy singing the lead vocal.

In seventy-six we left Pentyrch. It wasn't an easy decision I had lived there for thirteen years and had known it since first meeting Mary in school, and of course she was 'Pentyrch born and bred' but it was she who chose our new home. The move stemmed from the fact that the council had given us the option to buy 19 Danyrodyn at four thousand pounds but the house had its limitations. It was part of a terrace and though the back garden was large there was little chance of building an extension. Coupled with this the car had to be left on the road and though it was a cul-de-sac then, there were plans to continue the road into the field where they would, and did build more houses.

It was hard to leave Netta and Tom who were now in their late seventies but we arrange things so that they could move into our house on which I'd spent some time altering and decorating, and of course there was the telephone so that we could keep in touch. Tom felt it more than Netta so that if my car was outside, he'd come looking for me. On these occasions I was usually trying to record something which could only be done when Mary was at work and the children in school so I did my best to be diplomatic and after chatting for a while. I explained that where we were to live was only five miles over the mountain and that he'd past it when he'd worked for a short time at the Cwm colliery in Beddau, either walking over the Soar or using his bicycle.

Netta was still working in the occasional house but it seemed that much of her time was spent chatting and drinking tea. She also liked making her elderflower wine which could 'take the varnish off the piano'. No, but it was pretty strong. One day after finishing work I went to their house. "Look at this" she said taking a tea towel off a large earthenware bowl to reveal the wine with pieces of toast and lemon floating on the top. "Look at working" she said with pride as a bubble escaped through the 'flotsam'. She took a bottle out of the pantry and poured me a glass which I drank quite quickly before leaving. At home I washed in preparation for my tea only to look in the mirror to see my face red and glowing. My first thought was that I was allergic to the soap but no, that wine had quickly entered my blood stream through my empty stomach. In her lifetime Netta had done many things in the village including the collection of newspapers (salvage) during the war and arranging bus trips. Apart from delivering babies she'd been called upon to sit with the dying and to 'lay out' the dead. She had once been a member of Horeb Chapel where she had sent Mary but something had happened in the distant past that stopped her going. Perhaps this was demonstrated by an incident that I witnessed. It was a lovely summers day when a little girl came up the road who'd obviously been crying. Her eyes were red and her cheeks were smudged and she was one of four daughters who lived across the road and it was obvious to all there was little money in the household. When Netta asked her, what had upset her she replied that she'd been sent home from The Mission church because she was dirty? Netta waited on her step for an hour until the Sunday school teacher who was not far off the same age passed at the bottom of the street. She went down the road to confront her the words echoing "Call yourself a Christian, do you?" Perhaps something similar had happened at Horeb. She also had a great knowledge of herbal medicines with a natural cure for most things and Mary thought she would write some of these down. Tom had a condition of the eye left after bell's palsy perhaps and when we called in one day he was dancing about the room in pain. Instead of using Olive oil on his eye she'd used camphorated oil! Mary had second thoughts, maybe it was too late to ask her about those herbal remedies. Netta died in nineteen eighty-four aged eighty-seven and Tom the following year also aged eighty-seven.

So, we had moved to Crown Hill, Llantwit Fardre with Mac, Vaughan and Glyn Willicombe acting as removal men to a semi built in the late sixties complete with a garage. The estate was well known to us as we had visited Mary's cousin, Elaine and her husband regularly, and had been out with them and their neighbours to various functions. This house was nine thousand pounds and it was something of a stretch to find the deposit but Mum and Dad came to the rescue. My brother had continued to live at home until nineteen seventy while striving to pass his exams in accountancy which meant, at the time, passing nine topics, auditing, bookkeeping etc in one exam. If you failed one you had to take all nine once again. This proved challenging and he'd taken courses some residential, until he was successful. My parents had been constant in their support, which was sometimes financial and now they wanted to give something to us. Dad had been retired for five years but such was the nature of his job and the contractors he employed in the supply of materials, to the steelworks, there were always small rewards such as a turkey at Christmas which he received until the day he died. I can remember accompanying him in the car at Christmas as a ten-year-old delivering Christmas Boxes of cigarettes and liquor. He told me explicitly what I had to say when the door was answered, first the name "Mr So and So?" "Yes?" hand over the package and leave, don't accept anything that may be offered, while all the time Dad waited in the car the motor running. And so, the gears of industry were greased. When he finished work the car that he had driven was returned to the Steel Works and the next day a new car arrived curtesy of a major contractor. The solicitor was a little surprised when I handed over nine hundred pounds in cash, ten percent, but he said nothing.

In nineteen seventy-seven Mum Died. She had a heart condition brought on by having diphtheria as a child but it only seemed to affect her in her later years. When the heart malfunctioned and her lungs would fill up with fluid she'd go into hospital where her lungs would be drained. This happened once or twice a year and once home she would carry on as usual even though she'd suffer from a shortage of breath. Her attitude when she was told to take things easy was very much that if she couldn't scrub the kitchen floor then she may as well stop living. Dad would take her to different locations in the car where he'd listen to cassettes of choirs while Mum sketched and when she went into hospital for the last time it was only when the specialist asked to see us that I realised how ill she was. When I saw her for the last time, she'd had a stroke and was uncontrollably restless not knowing anyone. Aunty Lyn was already there and said "Here's Rod?" Mum stopped and looked at me and in that moment all the memories came flooding back to me and perhaps to her as well. She was sixty-six years old and when I think of the way in which heart valves are changed in a way that seems routine today, I can't help thinking that if she had only lived a little longer. Dad carried on living at Heol Ifor and resisted attempts by us to have him live with us or at least near us our thinking being that Jeremy and Sarah might prove a distraction from what could be a lonely life. He had also lost his brother, Uncle Walter and his good friend Emlyn Lloyd but Uncle Harold and Aunty Leah visited and Mac was only a few miles away in Rhiwbina, coupled with this George Raybould continued to make his weekly Saturday night visits.

We settled in without any problems with Sarah starting at Ysgol Gynradd Garth Olwg quickly making friends, one being Sarah Batten daughter of Molly and Roy who lived next door but one and after a year she met up her friends from Pentyrch at Ysgol Gyfun Llanhari. Jeremy however, found things a little difficult. He'd started at Radyr which he had enjoyed but now found it difficult to acclimatise to a new school where to begin with his accent made him a stranger. In hindsight we didn't give as much thought as we should have to this when we chose our new house, but eventually he overcame the difficulties making friends on the estate and the fact that he played drums and some guitar also helped him fit in.

Our next-door neighbours for a few years, Alan and Avril proved pleasant and amiable. Avril making a cake for us for my mother's funeral, preserving an old Welsh custom. On the other side were Bert and Nan. Bert had taken over the running of The Ship public house and to begin with had maybe two girlfriends but eventually Nan, his wife returned and after speaking to Mary decided to stay. Also in the street was Robert Saunders from Abercanaid and his wife Bridget, his father being a close friend of Uncle Harold so it was not surprising to have Uncle Harold visit us.

The street elected to have a jubilee party at which I was asked to play music through my amplifier and speakers.

Rodger and Caroline moved in across the road and became good friends. One day while working in the garden Caroline passed on her way home from work and I asked her how she was settling in. It seemed they weren't too happy so I invited them over for coffee and within two minutes Rodger was with us closely followed by Caroline. It turned out that he and Mary were related and that Dick Smith, Roy's father was Rodger's uncle. Rodger and Caroline were instrumental in our first flight and visit abroad when the four of us went to Ibiza and an unforgettable holiday.

I continued being self-employed while Mary worked firstly at Rizla and then Rediffusion and we settled into a contented way of life among many friends. Vaughan and Lorna arrived on Crown Hill as did Mary's cousin Julia Willicombe and Dewi Hughes who also taught at Pentyrch with his wife Heulwen.

I built a studio firstly in the garage and then an independent one on land at the back of the garage. A few years later we built one in Vaughan's attic where we recorded some of his ideas. He and Lorna would often come to our gigs, with Jeremy now playing drums, and socially it was a happy time but work-wise Vaughan had become impatient and after being overlooked for promotion at Pentyrch he decided to leave for a new position at St. Michaels Catholic School. He had also become warden, a leader of Pontypridd Gateway Club which provided social activities for people of all ages with learning difficulties, a part time job meeting one evening a week at a local special school. He asked me to go along with my guitar and it was something I really enjoyed and after a few weeks he offered me a job. When I said that I didn't want payment he replied, "One evening when there's frost on the ground or it's pouring with rain you'll think 'I won't bother to go tonight' but because you're getting paid, however small the wage you'll feel obliged to go". And he was right.

Mary enjoyed the Club and came along with me every Thursday night as a volunteer but because I was being paid, they sent the head of music for South Glamorgan schools to vet me. I'd recorded some songs of the day and as they played, I stood in front with my guitar encouraging the members to sing. Later I told that him this seemed to be the best way but asked him if he had any other ideas. "Don't ask me" he said. "I haven't got a clue." Vaughan told me when he'd left that he worked with the best young instrumentalists in the county. We were working towards appearing on stage at the Gateway Festival when with Mary's help and Shelia another volunteer we managed to get all of the members on stage, much to the delight of the parents of those who lived at home. Some of course lived in hostels. After another year Vaughan was once again unhappy at St. Michaels and had applied successfully to Millfield Junior School (Egerton Hall) to be a teacher and he and Lorna would be house parents there. When he told the parents that he was leaving they suggested that I would become leader to which he replied "Rod's only an electrician!" And Jesus only a carpenter. This was unbeknown to me but those parents made sure that I became leader. We were part of Tonyrefail Youth Wing and the Community Tutor suggested I did a part time youth leadership course which included some residential weekends to achieve the necessary qualifications.

We continued to take part in the yearly festivals and sports competitions which took part on weekends which rankled with the teachers I employed because none of us got paid. Volunteers were much better but unfortunately it was easier to employ teachers who were already qualified and I tried hard to pick those who I thought could have some fondness for the job, perhaps vocational in the way they viewed it.

At the beginning of seventy-eight Mary's Aunty Doris phoned telling me that her step-mother and Mary's step-grandmother Gwladys, had died and that her council flat was empty except for the pedal organ which was there for me to pick up! I liked playing it when we visited her and apparently, I'd mentioned that after her days I would like it and she had not forgotten. So, with Vaughan, who had an estate car we brought it over to Crown Hill where it proved to be quit inspirational. Our ideal life however, took a hit when Avril and Alan moved out and the 'Roffies' moved in. They were continually fighting and though we weren't joined to them like poor Molly and Roy it was disconcerting living with the ever-present threat of violence. On one occasion a fight broke out between the wife's father and her husband when I went in, followed by a neighbour the father who had been beaten dropped a knife in the kitchen sink.

Through another contact I met Dave Williams who had a studio in Purley, Surrey and we recorded some tracks using the organ/harmonium one of which was Rainbow Waters. It was originally a song but he saw it as an instrumental which he eventually recorded using the Strawbs but their name couldn't be used on the record due to contractual problems and so the fictitious band Driftwood appeared on the label and it was released in seventy-nine on Dave's Jig-Saw label. Sue, Dave's wife worked hard on promoting it narrowly missing the required number of radio stations who were playing it at the same time to enable it to appear in the trade paper The Music Week whereby the retailer would stock it so that it would be on the shelf should someone ask for it. (If it appeared on the Radio One or Two playlist It would automatically be listed). It was an eye opener for me as to how the system worked. It was played regularly on Radio Wales and as background music on an HTV sports programme, it also had releases in Italy and Holland and Belgium but the fact that the Strawbs name couldn't be used tended to hold it back.

Family holidays were spent at Bournemouth, New Quay and at Tenby where we had the last holiday with Dad. Kiln Park was also a favourite when holidays were spent with the likes of Lyndon and Lynette, Elain and Derek and Geoff and Diane. A few years later Jeremy met up with Brian Conoley who was performing there. He'd met him earlier when he was part of the comedy group Tom Foolery and when they were looking for a novelty song they had come to the house and we'd put some ideas down in the studio. Jeff, the leader of the group became a good friend and Mary and me often visited he and Meryl in Ebbw Vale. He had a recording studio which I used and later a Pizza parlour called Pizza Pan where I did some electrical work. Then the group graciously performed a charity gig at Rhydfelen Labour Club to raise funds for the Gateway Club which was a sell-out and a great night was had by all who came. Y Diliau had recorded Pitar Pan and about this time I met Frank again who was working for CBC, a forerunner of Red Dragon and he persuaded me to let him interview me where he played that, and some of the old releases I'd had. When I got home Mary, and others couldn't believe my 'Cardiff' accent which was down to Frank's influence and my time in the steel works.

At this time Radio One had come to Cardiff as part of a regional campaign and the DJ chose to play Pitar Pan which must have been the first time that a Welsh language record was played on Radio One.

Mac had moved to Pen-y-dre in Rhiwbina where the twins Ruth and Nathan were born and later to Wenallt Road so that between us we could keep an eye on Dad but by the early eighties he started to have Petit Mal's, mini seizures and because he smoked, holes started to appear in his shirt and waistcoat. We decided that a trial period in a residential home might be the answer and as Mac's business partner had bought one at Porthcawl we asked Dad if he would like to try it. As he seemed to settle there, we took the opportunity to move to Bridgend which was nearer the home and nearer to the company where I worked. At about this time my self-employed work became scant and I found employment as a supervisor/electrician with a contracting firm. This also gave us the excuse to leave the Roffies and the ever-present threat of things 'kicking off' as they often did.

Prior to this I'd written I Have Seen It All which Dave Williams liked and we recorded it at Stacy Road, a studio owned by the BBC. We were trying to get a Salvation Army sound and John Leach who was known to Mac and me assembled the musicians among them Lawrence Davies a trumpet player that I'd met on various Disc a Dawn sessions. Unfortunately, on the day of the recording he wasn't available and another trumpeter who wasn't really good enough took his place. I played the organ and the Silurian Male Voice Choir also took part in what was in the main an enjoyable experience.

Dave tried hard to get a release and almost succeeded when a company called Ritz Records were interested until the last minute when internal wrangling put a stop to it being released.

When Dad became ill, we took him to a specialist who wanted more tests done but his condition worsened quite rapidly and he died at the Heath Hospital where Mum had died some six years earlier. Netta had died leaving Tom at Rhiwfelin Nursing home so we decided to return to Llantwit Fardre. The two years that I'd spent working for the company were a nightmare in as much as the electricians who were on 'piecework' left things unfinished so that many times I was responsible for completion as well as doing my work as a supervisor. And so, when the opportunity came to leave, I left.

One of the houses at The Paddocks, Church Village was used as a Show House and because I'd been to the site with the firm I asked if we could buy it and after barely a year in Bridgend we moved in to the house.

The garage was used as the sales office and as it was a good corner plot, we extended it so that the office became another living-room and we built a garage which was attached to it. Jeremy and me did a great deal of the work putting in footings and the like and we employed a bricklayer who lived down the road. Then, Tom died and we realised that because I was now out of work except for a small monthly remuneration for my Gateway work, and also Mary who had some trouble with her nerves probably due to the deaths that came one after the other, we found ourselves at 'a crossroads.' Sarah was attending a BTech course at Rhydfelen and Jeremy a course at a skill-centre in Port Talbot so Mary and me decided to look for a sub post office which we found at Bryn, Port Talbot. Jeremy who had been playing bass guitar for a few years was asked to play in a cabaret band called Illusion the leader of which coincidentally, was Brian John, part of Dormouse who I'd taken up to Rockfield in nineteen-seventy. Brian couldn't understand why we were leaving a new detached house to live in the village of Bryn where he'd performed in the rugby club, but 'needs must' and in October eighty-six we moved.

Before we left Jeremy and me recorded a couple of tracks for a compilation album to be released by Sain, probably the last vinyl album they released. It was called Valley Lights, a song by Frank who was also on the album and it was recorded using their mobile studio which came down to a church at St Andrews Place in Cardiff. I sang and played the organ, which we took with us and Jeremy played bass. The songs were, I Have Seen It All and my original English version of Cael Cymru Rydd on which I was delighted to have Heather Jones who was also recording that day sing a verse and join me on the choruses. The record didn't sell that well but I remember hearing Cael Cymru Rydd on the car radio as I travelled from Bryn to the Gateway Club in Talbot Green. Regretfully I finished almost ten years after I'd become their leader. Before we left Lyndon and me played at an anti-nuclear rally at Sophia Gardens, Cardiff. The organizers and the crowd marched down from the royal ordinance factory at Caerphilly Road where people like Dafydd Iwan, Heather and ourselves performed on the back of a lorry. One of the speakers was Tony Robinson (Sir) would you believe, and the brilliant Gwyn Alf Williams.

The lady who ran the post office was on her own since her husband had left but she had a boyfriend and two children, one out of school and the other in his last year. Fortunately for us she had little interest in the office or the house so we were able to buy it well below her asking price but it did need much work. A terraced, two bedroomed house with an upstairs bathroom and the post-office in the 'front room' meant that we needed a third bedroom. Jeremy, who'd been living with Peter, a member of the Brian's band came home and together we built a 'double decker' that is a new kitchen with a new bedroom above. Sarah finished off her course at Bridgend college and Jeremy bought a carpet cleaning machine and became self-employed. While we did the building work Mary, who had someone from the post office with her for two weeks quickly picked up the running of the office and with her personality those who had chosen to have their pension else ware returned to the post office. This had happened because the previous post mistress who was from the village and a divorcee had spent much time in the local club and some people wrongly assumed that she could be breaking their confidences. Once the extension had been built Mary convinced me that I should also learn the post office routine and so I was able to help out on busy 'pension mornings' and then share the work when only one of us was needed.

For fifteen out of the seventeen years we spent in the post office things were good. We had an annual holiday paid for by the post office who had a head office in Swansea. We were usually successful in finding someone to relieve for us while we took our two-week holiday which was usually Pembroke or Cardigan meeting Howard and his family, or Cornwall and Tenerife. Later we bought a small flat in Pentyrch where we could spend our weekends often having someone to relieve for us on Saturday mornings. We sold greetings cards, wrapping paper and stationery which had a regular turnover and we also tried chocolates but the margins were too small. We sold wool and Mary being a knitter herself enjoyed conversations and giving advice to fellow knitters in the village who bought wool. The demise of the post office began when it was decided to introduce cards instead of pension books. Prior to this our customers would collect their pension, invalidity benefits or family allowance in cash once a week out of which they would purchase saving stamps for gas, electricity, telephone, motor vehicle and TV licence. We received payment for the stamps that we sold then, they would return with their bill and saving stamps when it was due. Once cards were introduced all these transactions disappeared.

Music-wise when we had finished the extension, we converted a third of the garage into a studio which housed the organ, a Korg keyboard, my reel-to-reel Tascam and a mixer, curtesy of Jeff (Tomfoolery). We had recorded three tracks for the Vally Lights album but only two had been used the third one was called Before the Strangers Came. I had written this when I thought back to Pentyrch as a village with a small population where everyone knew everyone else to the small town it had become. Robin 'picked up' on this and when he translated it, he thought of the problems in Gwynedd where he was from where homes were being bought up by strangers, sometimes holiday homes and the actions of Meibion Glyndwr through the eighties. It was now called Cyn I'r Dieithriaid Ddod. "Roedd croeso'n Llwyn 'Reos,Llain Delyn a'r Hafod,a ffid yn Tros'Rafon a'r Bryn A chlust i bob problem ar aelwyd Llwyn Rhuddem, a phanad o de yn Y Glyn Ond gwag yw aelwydydd Rose Cottage, Green Gables The Nook a Mon Repose A rhyw wythnos yn ol roedd Chez Nous ar dan yn goelcerth yn g'leuo'r nos"

"A welcome at Llwyn'Reos,'Llain Delyn and Hafod,Tros 'Rafon and Y Bryn. An ear for a problem at the home of Llwyn Rhuddem and a cup of tea at Y Glyn Empty homes empty names Rose Cottage, Green Gables, The Nook and Mon Repose, And a week ago was it Chez Nous on fire? like a beacon in the night"

This was nineteen-ninety and we originally wanted Bryn Fon to sing it but when I telephoned him, he apologised but explained that his guitarist also had a song in the competition which he was going to sing. As we finished our conversation and I was about to replace the receiver I heard what sounded like the rewind of a tape recorder so it was obvious that Special Branch were still tracking him after his spurious arrest and anyone else who called him. On the a news broadcast a detective had shown the news-crew some wires and batteries as he picked them out of a lose brick in the wall of Bryn's house!

When I talked to a retired policeman on the plane to Tenerife he confirmed my suspicions, that firstly the area would have been taped off, then the people from forensics if not the bomb squad would have been called before anyone would have been allowed to touch them.

We came third in the competition; the song Bryn sang coming first but we enjoyed meeting up with Marged and others on our overnight stop in Gwynedd. Robin had also been to Bryn where they had filmed inserts to use in the programme, some being filmed in my studio and also outside in the village. In ninety-one we watched the Richard Williams Junior singers perform Pitar Pan which was televised from the Urdd Eisteddfod. The programme was introduced by the tenor Stuart Boroughs and though the tempo was a little different the audience seemed to enjoy it.

In ninety-two Dafydd Iwan sang I Gael Cymru'n Gymru Rydd on a TV programme entitled Can I Gymru Ddoe a Heddw, and is probably the best version to date.

Those times I wasn't needed in the office and no chores were outstanding (I could clean and do the ironing but was hopeless at cooking), I was happy in my studio and In nineteen-nighty Vaughan asked me to expand on an idea I had had many years before for a children's musical. It was about Caradog and his heroic defence of his Silurian land when the Romans invaded Wales. He wanted to perform at Millfield prep school and in that year Mary and me went down to Somerset to see it performed. Then in ninety-four Mary's cousin Julia (Willicombe) who was a music teacher at Llanedyrn High decided to use it at her school which I enjoyed immensely, performed over three nights the children of up to fifteen years of age who might have been lacking in technique certainly made up for with enthusiasm and the show went down well with the audiences, even though it was something of a deprived area. After I'd said a few words complimenting the cast and the musicians the headmaster thanked everyone especially those who were looking after the cars in the carpark!

At about this time I decided to write or translate one of my songs into Welsh. I had made suggestions that Robin had used in some translations, but when it came to others, he was the poet. I chose a song called It's Easy to Say Nothing which translated to Mae'n Hawdd. Mae'n hawdd bod yn anwybodus, 'anwybodus' translated as ignorant, so 'it's easy to be ignorant' and using an 'odliadur' and many phrases I'd picked up during the years, I sent it up to Dafydd Iwan at Sain and was so pleased when Iola and Andy recorded it on their CD, but not without some changes by the producer! It was released in ninety-seven, on a CD entitled Cerdded Dros Y Mynedd. The writer was Rhodri Thomas and I received his royalties by mistake so I sent him a cheque only to be told by the PRS that he wasn't a member. Oops!

At the beginning of that year Vaughan arrived at the post office. He wanted to organise yet another performance of the musical (Children of the Oak, which he wanted to call Caradog) with his then current crop of students. We discussed the changes that he wanted to make, one of them being that it would be longer which meant four more new songs around alterations in the plot. He also wanted a CD to sell to parents and to this end he used a composer of film music called Mark Thomas who lived in Swansea and had recently written the music for the film Twin Town. The connection was that the director of the film was the brother of the actor Keith Allen and as his daughter Lily was one of the cast. When I visited Mark at his studio most of the tracks were complete and he just needed my guitar on some and my Walkabout Dulcimer on another, later Vaughan brought a mini-bus of children up from Millfield to record the vocals. The CD was sold to parents but even though the recording and the production of the it was rushed it was still not available until after the show had finished its run. However, we enjoyed our visit down to Somerset to see one of the performances.

In ninety-nine Sarah married Roger Jones. She had always had an independent side to her nature and after spending three months working in Greece in the early nineties, she came home to find a job which would suit her qualifications. She shared a flat in Cardiff with her then boyfriend but when she bought her house in Pontypridd, she decided to charge him rent rather than add him to the mortgage. The next boyfriend was an insurance assessor who lived at home with his parents and was not an easy character to read. It ended when unbeknown to us he had struck her and it was many years later when we discovered that Jeremy had addressed this act and was dragged of him before doing any serious damage. While working at Welsh Water she met Roger whose marriage was ending when his wife had been seeing someone else but while the wife had custody of his three children they invariably spent much of their time with Roger, and Sarah was happy to accommodate them. The marriage was special and took place at a hotel in Cwmbran where we invited all our friends and close relatives and she came down the aisle, if you can call it that in a civil wedding, to the strains of Fly Me to The Moon.

Also, in this year Jeremy wrote and recorded some great tracks in a studio in Cornwall. In the eighties he'd recorded some tracks for Black Mountain and then for Kingsley at Rockfield as a bass player, but these were his and the management promised great things but eventually they came to nothing.

In two-thousand I sent one of the new songs, Travel The Road that I'd written for the musical to Richard Williams at Tonyrefail. He was dedicated to music and had bought the house next door to where he lived specifically for the use of the three choirs he ran, with a little help from his daughters. He was in his eighties then and had started his illustrious career in music as a boy soprano and had toured with the Ovaltinies concert party a choir set up to promote this product in the nineteen-thirties and was heard regularly on broadcasts from Radio Luxemburg. He worked hard with the choir's male, mixed and children but on the night of a concert would adopt a leisurely stance against the piano from where he would conduct. The children took to the song immediately and we saw it performed a number of times most notably at St Davids Hall, Cardiff at a concert in aid of the charity, Scope. I received an unexpected phone call from his daughter who told me that on their visit to Austria they had sang it in their repertoire at Salzburg before travelling to other venues but on their return found that the local choir had learnt it and it became a joint performance at the end of the evening, and their trip to Austria.

You write a song for yourself initially trying to put your idea down in the best way you can and hope that it makes a connection to other people. The more people that make that connection the happier you are. During that year they produced a CD and Travel the Road was among the titles. As time passed, Mary obtained more benefits for customers who she could see were missing out, a carers allowance for those who were struggling to look after someone and also supplementary allowances they could apply for.

At one time she had to visit the doctor who with all good intention was giving out information which wasn't applicable to everyone without knowing the patient's particular circumstances as regards to their pensions.

Her work did not go unnoticed and she received many gifts which she would reluctantly accept and invitations to the rugby club for various celebrations in the village and she soon made many friends. She decided to learn how to swim and took lessons and when she encouraged a friend who was petrified of the water to join her the friend described her as 'my hero'. She also had some inside information on a house which had been repossessed and was instrumental in Jeremy buying that house.

One event which served to give us some realisation of the job we were in happened one summer evening when she was about to lock up and robbers entered the post office. She had the presence of mind to press the alarm button which apart from ringing outside was deafening in the office and sent the robbers fleeing empty handed. Jeremy and me had been in the kitchen and chased after them but were stopped in our tracks when one of the robbers pointed a gun at us. That night when I held her in my arms, she sobbed a little when we got to bed, but come the morning she was back behind the counter.

When we bought the flat in Pentyrch, Mary loved being back in the village and meeting friends old and new spending time in the Lewis Arms particularly when Jeremy played with his friend Wills as a duo. Auntie Doris was still in her bungalow with Haydn and was delighted to have Mary back and as they were getting older Mary did many things for her which prompted a friend of Doris to say "I wish I had a Mary!"

When Sarah declared that she was pregnant Mary immediately felt it was time to move permanently to Pentyrch nearer to Sarah particularly when Sarah and Roger sold their house in Cwmbran and moved to Church Village. In 2001 after our first grandson Eli was born, we decided to sell the post office but first there was a trip to Texas.

Mary had thought about tracing her GI father more out of curiosity than anything else and with a name like Othmar Jarisch he wasn't too hard find. She enlisted the help of a Colonel Grinton who had much success in finding GI fathers who had fought in Vietnam, Korea and WW2 and he actually lived in the Santa Rosa area of California. It turned out that Othmar had died in 1987 but Grinton personally knew his widow Peggy and he proceeded to tell her about Mary! Someone she knew nothing about!

"She didn't take it too well" he explained. Were we surprised? No.

During the next couple of years Mary had telephone conversations with her. She could be interesting, talking about her job as a school teacher before she retired and that Othmar had been working in animal welfare.

Other times she was vindictive. She had contacted an old army buddy to find out if it was true. We found out later that it was the cartoonist creator Charles Schulz who had used the name Miss Othmar for a school teacher character in his cartoon strip Peanuts. Othmar and Peggy had no children and Mary believes that she turned up at the post office one day but did not make herself known. But we were now going to Texas to visit Othmar's sister, Mary's Aunt Dolie. Peggy had said that Othmar was from Texas and relocated to California after the war had ended but that he had relations in New Braunfells, where he was born and Mary's search found Dolie who was delighted that she had made contact and after much correspondence and telephone calls a visit was tentatively arranged. I say tentatively because Mary did not want to put Dolie to the trouble of putting us up.

After leaving the peaks of Snowdon poking through the mist some nine hours later, we were looking down on the sparseness of Greenland, then Canada and finally we arrived at Chicago. A huge airport and after dropping our luggage off we caught the shuttle to the terminal for Austin. The plane was smaller and it was a somewhat bumpy ride with a lot of low cloud and it was impossible to see anything for a while. I imagined the pilot with his feet up and using auto pilot, then when eventually it cleared, we could see scattered houses below until we landed there. Fortunately, no frisks or detectors that we'd experienced at Chicago and soon we were outside picking up a taxi for the Embassy Suites Hotel.

In the meantime, Peggy had died in California and the next-door neighbour who had cleaned out the house where she'd lived had come across letters that Mary had sent. The neighbour could not believe this of Othmar who she'd known since she was a little girl and it was all the more poignant because she and her husband were about to adopt a little girl. From the goodness of her heart, she sent Mary a box of things that she thought would be of interest, photo's, a veteran's flag, epaulettes from his uniform and some drawings by Charles Schulz commemorating Othmar's birthday. Indeed, it seems that it was Schulz who may have been responsible for Othmar locating to Santa Rosa, when relations with his parents in New Braunfels, had broken down after Mary's birth. Dolie who was Othmar's youngest sister was thirteen at the time and can remember the disquiet in the deeply protestant family at Othmar's actions. We felt jet-lagged and slept for most of the day then went down to the restaurant in the evening. It was happy hour and after Mary went back up to our room, I spent a few hours talking to an Irishman and a Geordie who were taking an Intel course and had similar feelings to me about 'the English', and Mrs Thatcher. The barman's family were also Welsh and he asked me if I knew the Jones'? It was very much like the TV series called Cheers.

On successive days we went to a mall, to Barton Springs Pool which was a natural rock pool which had been turned into a public amenity, it felt cold but then it was over 80 degrees before we got in. We visited the Bob Bullock Museum where we spent the day looking at everything from the prehistoric, the native Americans, the Spanish and the Texans. The 'Dillo's were great.

Small free electric buses which would drop you anywhere on route.

The river ran alongside the hotel, the lesser Colorado, and at dusk people would arrive to watch the bats emerging from under the Congress bridge over the river. In the day there was always something to see on the river walk, a small log with a bird, two turtles and a heron perched on it and people jogging sometimes pushing baby buggies. On the day we arrived the Congress Bridge had been closed to traffic before the beginning of a road race the obligatory anthem was sung with hands on hearts, by a female country singer.

Sixth Street by day was unassuming but by night was bouncing. After visiting an acoustic bar, we found Kenny Lunes, and his grand piano, radio mike and drummer who launched into Great Balls Of Fire. Incredible. He asked where we were from and when we said Wales, he played It's Not Unusual. People put requests and dollars into a jar on the piano. We left about 12.30, passed a guy with star-shaped glasses singing and playing a bass! The sound of Dixieland jazz from another bar, a girl in a dress! Hang on he's got a beard!

Lots of couples out walking in what was a really friendly atmosphere.

At the end of the week, we headed for New Braunfels some thirty miles south of Austin to meet Dolie. We had booked the 'Texas Cottage' in Cormal Avenue, and we were not disappointed as it had everything we needed.

```
EGON (99 years)                    brother to                    OTHMAR(Snr)

|                                                                      |
---------------------------------------------------------          -_____
Bennet      Louella      Tressie      Janet      Othmar   Dolie  Elizabeth
|           |            |            |          |        |      hus,Hanno
Butch       Steven+Thresa                        Mary     Carol,Debbie
partner                                                    partner
Sandy                                                       Roger
```

After meeting the owners, Ellen, the cleaner took us in her car to the super market, she was from New York and when she met Butch, she said "You're German aren't you I can tell by your blue eyes!" He was about fifth generation with black hair and looked like Jeremy! His girlfriend was Sandy and when we met her father, he spoke German as did Egon who was proud to say that he could speak German, Spanish and English. With them was Dolie and Louella. They were slim and Dolie was a youthful seventy and her looks belied her age. She was tall for a woman with grey hair and wore slacks. Louella was shorter and walked with a limp after having polio as a child and they were both widows. Mary and Louella had written to each other and we were the same age. Sandy who worked for a cement company and looked after the welfare of immigrant, workers, wanted to know how Mary and Dolie were related and when Othmar's name was mentioned I diplomatically explain that he was 19years of age in a foreign country and that it's water under the bridge. Dolie with tears in her eyes says "He shouldn't have done that". It was a moving moment. The six of us went out for a meal where we met Louella's sisters Tressie and Janet. Mary and Dolie really got on well together, going outside for a cigarette and a chat every now and then.

After the meal we drove to Dolie's bungalow. It seemed old fashioned with a lot of wood panelling and alongside it a small building that contained a pump which drew water from an artesian well underground. In summer when the Water-Park was open thousands of people visited the town.

We met Elizabeth who had visited Othmar but she was reluctant to get into conversation with us unlike second husband, Hanno who at 86 was a fireman, and Carpenter and was proud of his boat. Dolie still worked and it seemed that no one thought of themselves as being particularly old. Hanno was interesting and was most interested in us as was Roger who played in a band and recorded people in his spare time. Rap-Gospel at the time!

Sunday morning Butch and Sandy picked us up and took us to a park where tables had been laid out and food arranged including a cake made in honour of Mary's visit. They'd really gone to town on it. There were so many relatives who wanted to talk to us and because we were 'in demand' Mary and me didn't get to talk until we were back at the Texan cottage.

The next day Butch and Dolie took us to San Antonio and the Alamo. Butch had been married twice and worked at picking up wrecks. He has a son and had a mother living in New York who died a year ago. In the past he'd worked up there as a Private Investigator and was sometimes placed in companies to discover fraud and theft. Now he picks up the occasional wreck but has two guys working for him and also has a mobile-home park on land given to him by Egon.

At the Alamo we saw the Draig Goch among the other flags indicating that a Welshman, Lewis Johnson died at the battle. There was everything from flint arrow heads to musket balls powder horns and moulds, Crockett's flintlock and Bowie's knife and at the gift shop guns from a derringer to a colt 45. There was a 2.2 rifle exactly as I had had as a child the only difference being this one was real. I explained to Butch and some guys standing by about arms restrictions in the UK, the one translating to the other in Spanish. Dolie's husband sold guns and Butch had rifles and hand guns. He also had a licence to carry one from his PI days. The San Antonio River runs in a canal through San Antonio with shops and businesses either side and after a boat trip on the canal we settled down in the Hard Rock Cafe for lunch where Dolie said "A vegie-burger! What's a vegie-burger?" She didn't pick up on this however, as the following evening when we had a meal at her house with her daughters and their partners she served real shepherds-pie. Butch looked at Mary who wasn't a 'vegie' and smiled as I ate it without saying a word. When someone asked a waitress what she would recommend for a vegetarian she said "Get out of Texas!"

Butch took us to Luckenbach with Janet and Tressie who took calls on her cell phone from someone looking after her Bail Bond Agency. On the way out of New Braunfels we stopped at Tressie's daughters who lived in a fine brick-built house which according to Butch was the result of someone defaulting on a bail-bond. She had rescued a faun which was quite tame and was trying to protect it from predators and hunters I suppose. Luckenbach was somewhere we wanted to visit after seeing a Jerry Jeff Walker concert from the dance hall there on video. Apart from this there were many smaller type houses all made of wood one a post office and shop selling CD's and gifts and a couple of guys singing and playing guitars. There was also what I assume was once a toilet on which was a sign MOBILE PHONE BOX. We met the mayor who was also the sheriff and chatted to customers, one who had lived in the UK for a while and his mother who was visiting from Germany and spoke little English but smiled and left us with 'aufwiedersehen.'

Fredericksburg where we stopped for lunch was neat and tidy. They say that if the police find any vagrants there, they take them seventy miles down to San Antonio and drop them off. We passed by the LBJ Ranch with his herd of bison. Flags everywhere with God bless America on them.

Tressie asked if one of us could talk to her Rotary Club about Wales?

During a sudden hailstone shower where the hail seemed to be the size of large marbles Butch stopped under an under-pass to avoid his pick-up being dented.

I spoke at the Rotary Club that evening and everyone seemed interested. I had to dispel some myths informing them that the Prince and Princess of Wales were really nothing to do with the Welsh people but as I spoke, I got the feeling that the English treatment of the Welsh was akin to the US governments treatment of the native Americans and so I toned it down. Many questions including many about the Welsh language. I think Tressie was pleased.

York Creek was the home of Dolie's family when she was young and she remembered swimming in the creek with Othmar, she was disappointed to see a ploughed field in its place. Bennet had researched the family from their origins in the German speaking Czech area, Sudetenland maybe, and their arrival in the eighteen hundreds and took us to see the graves of Othmar Snr and his parents. Bennet belonged to group that looked after these graves.

We enjoyed a meal at Tressie's mobile home with the police radio on in the background so that they could be on hand should anyone need to be bailed. She lived near Butch and looked out for him when Bennet's second wife, Shirley didn't much like him.

Sandy brought an apple pie and at the end of the evening said her goodbyes. She, like most of the family lived in bungalow type dwellings with zinc roofs that always had plenty of land around them. She had cats but had to beware of coyotes who would approach the property then roll on their backs to entice the cats out.

We took Egon home who seemed quite nimble for his age and then Butch showed us his mobile home park. About twenty buildings which looked like bungalows as screens covered their wheels. A guy and his family stopped on his way out to apologise for being late with his rent. Butch was laid-back and when the guy had left said to us "They're kind of hill billys you know?"

We visited Gruene the next day which had the oldest dance-hall in Texas and a huge antique store where we bought a colt 45, prop pistol for Jeremy. They told us we could mail it home at the post office but in the end, this proved to be too complicated and after a call to the airline we packed it away in our suitcase.

On the last day, we said goodbye to Dolie who was working and Butch and Louella insisted on taking us up to Austin and the Embassy Hotel where we spent the last night before leaving the next day for Chicago and then home. Two months after arriving home Egon died aged 99 and they wanted us to go back out for his funeral but when we thought about the arrangements we'd had to make for the last trip, the amount of work involved and finding a relief this seemed impossible. Tressie, Butch and the others even wanted to pay for our flight but after much thought we decided it was impractical.

In October 2002 Jeremy went over and enjoyed the time with his American family and it was somewhere where Mary and me always intended to return.

The collection of photographs from Texas are as follows: -

*THE TOP PHOTOGRAPH is of me on the stage at the dance hall in Luckenbach.*

*THE PHOTO ALONGSIDE is of Mary with great uncle Egon and 'the cake'. BELOW LEFT is a scene from the party in the park with Louella in foreground. ALONGSIDE is Mary, me and Dolie in front of the Alamo.*

*THE BOTTOM LEFT is a photo taken at Dolie's house of Dolie, Mary and me and Dolie's children and spouses.*

*ALONGSIDE is Butch. Tressie and Barbara*

Back home and an offer for the post office from a couple who lived in Devon. They loved the fact that from the front of the house was an uninterrupted view of the wooded slopes across the valley, which reminded them of Switzerland, and that walks through those woods would lead to Margam Park. The husband was from Wolverhampton originally and talked of a time when he was stationed in North Wales with the RAF and that there was a certain animosity towards them from the local inhabitants. I reassured him that his would-be customers could speak English but I didn't say how much I enjoyed conversing with those who spoke Welsh. We echoed the feelings of the post office that though things were changing there was still a future after pension books gave way to cards. In our hearts however we believed that profit now directed its future and the days of it being a vital part of a community would come to an end. When we arrived in the village there were three shops and the post office and passing through there were always people walking or chatting. The post office was the first 'port of call' for advertising events happening in the village and the funeral director would give notice of a coming funeral. Now there is just one shop. After about five years the people who bought the post office just closed it and left, selling it as a house. This decision was not forced upon them the salary and livelihood was still in place and a provision to earn more from the shop side of the business a real possibility. In truth they did not endear themselves to their customers the husband once putting the flag of St George outside the office on St Georges day. I remember some of our customers had been on picket duty during the miner's strike and the flag and Mrs Thatcher had the same connotation to many.

At first the flat seemed to be everything that we wanted and we enjoyed looking after our grandson and receiving visits from friends and relations particularly my brother and his wife who lived in Penarth. He'd had cancer but after treatment it now seemed to be in remission.

I had joined the local history society while living at Bryn but now it was easier to attend the monthly meetings and to my surprise Don Llewellyn, our chairman and Mary's relative, and Ellis Davies, one of the founder members called at the flat and asked me to be secretary of the society. I explained that I had no experience of such a position but Don assured me it would be in name only, which didn't turn out to be the case. I mentioned that I didn't even have a computer and the next day Ellis arrived with one complete with monitor which he'd made up of various parts. I discovered later on visits to his house that his garage contained lots of computers and their parts which he enjoyed tinkering with. He was a man in his seventies then but during his career had been all over the world working in the plastics industry and was actually credited with inventing the plastic cup. This was in two thousand and three and since then I have continued to book our speakers.

The flat on the other hand turned out to be more troublesome. When we visited on weekends it was quiet only because the man who lived above us went home to his family. Soon however various people occupied the rented flat, and it was me in particular who resented the noise above us and at one stage between occupants, and with the permission of the owner, I put sound insulation boards under the carpet but to no avail. The flats were timber framed and not conducive to a building such as that at all.

Also, in this year we celebrated our fortieth wedding anniversary, and a celebration that we were not expecting. We'd arranged to go out for a meal with Lyndon and Lynette but when we arrived at the Kings Arms in the village, I noticed my brother's personalised number plate and realised that something was afoot. Entering the saloon bar, we found all our friends and relations there.

Sarah and Jeremy who'd hired the bar had managed to keep the arrangements a secret almost until the last minute and it was an evening we very much enjoyed. The noise in the flat was bearable until the Australians arrived!

Two young men in their early twenties had been loosely employed to coach the rugby team and were to occupy the flat above us, and when they first appeared I knew we were in trouble arriving on the back of a pick-up truck which also contained mattresses.

A few weeks later I went up to reason with them complaining about the noise and explaining the short comings of the building and one of them was understanding but the other not. I was also astonished to see a mixture of eight or so young men and women there and decided it was time to leave.

Mac, had an accountancy practice at Dinas Powis but at the beginning of two-thousand and four and after it appeared that his cancer had been treated successfully at Llandough, he decided to retire. He looked forward to holding yet another of his legendary Christmas parties with his many friends and family but it was not to be, and as the year progressed it was obvious the cancer had returned and we spent many days chatting and remembering our childhood days, our holidays, our parents and their individual characteristics, the band members who had come and gone, football and of course our children and their futures.

*TOP. Howard, William, Elizabeth and Ann at the party. ALONGSIDE. Thehappy couple.*

*BELLOW. Mac and me awaiting Sara and Roger to Fly Me to The Moon. ALONGSIDE. Lorna, Heulwen and Vaughan with Elizabeth in front of him.BELLOW. Me, Doris and Haydn with Lynette in the foreground.*

*ALONGSIDE. Jeremy, Lyndon and his son Paul.*

*BELLOW. Doris, Haydn, Bev(standing) Mac (Beryl at back) Jeremy and Ruth.ALONGSIDE. Mary and Eli.*

Mac was very much like my father a Christian in his belief, upright and honest. He had called back to the office one evening only to find his business partner, who was married, in a compromising position with his secretary. He immediately took steps to end the partnership. He'd continued to be a member at Beulah long after I had left and one of the last things, we did together was attend a book launch about Rhiwbina which contained a photo of us in our skiffle days, and though he had difficulty in walking he enjoyed meeting old friends. At Llandough I sat alongside him together with Bev and Ruth when he died and in that moment all those shared memories were gone.

I acknowledged to a congregation full to capacity at Beulah that it was fitting, as it was here his life had begun and it was also here, we'd said goodbye to Dad.

At the crematorium Wyn Calvin an entertainer of the 'old school' gave a short eulogy about Mac's connection to the Variety Club as its treasurer and showing that in his heart he was always something of a performer.

It was January of two thousand and five and while I was grieving, we were told that our flat had sold and we were obliged to find some where to live fairly quickly. Fortunately, by this time the

Australians had left which made us feel easier in not having to burden the purchaser with their noise and once again we moved over the mountain to Chandlers Reach a stones-throw away from Crown Hill, Llantwit Fardre where we had lived some twenty years before.

We settled in immediately making friends with our new neighbours but in July I broke my leg while playing with Eli on Caerphilly Mountain. I'd picked him up and ran into the ferns shouting 'to infinity and beyond' not taking into account the slope in the ground below the ferns and when I 'braked' so that he would fall back on me I heard the crack. It took a few expletives on my part to convince Mary what had happened but eventually she contacted Sarah and Roger and after some painful waiting an ambulance took me to the Heath Hospital where they found I had broken the tibia and fibula as they entered my ankle. After two operations I was home and if I sat up in bed, I could see Jeremy building my small studio at a place we'd selected in the garden, and in a few months, I was able fit insulation and plasterboards while my leg was in a 'cage' which by November had been removed. Not long after we received a visit from cousin Alun Francis and was probably due to an e-mail, I had sent him regretting the fact that I didn't know about the death of his twin brother Gwyn. I had last seen them both at their father's funeral but I'd often called at the house where Gwyn and his mother lived but when there was no reply, a neighbour told me that Aunty Lyn was in a home and that Gwyn still lived there and was 'round and about somewhere'. As regards the Peter's side of the family I've mentioned Aunty Dil and Aunty Lyn but not Uncle Tom. I suppose it was because he moved out of the Merthyr valley to live in firstly Llanharan and then Bridgend. Here his three sons Leonard, Clive and Michel were born. Later all three worked at The Park when it was a psychiatric hospital Michael in the boiler house, Leonard in charge of maintenance and Clive as an electrician. I first met Clive or took notice of him when he was doing his national service and was based at the Maindy Barracks in Cardiff. It was only about four miles from us and he would occasionally visit us on his motor bike and stay for tea. He was already married and found life difficult to cope, which was something that stayed with him through-out his life. After finishing his national service my father found him a job at Llanharry Iron Ore Mine which was owned by the steel works, but in later life, when he would visit us at the post office, he told me how he was picked on and bullied there. When the Park became a prison and the original patients were supposed to be looked after in group homes, he found some shabbily dressed at the bus station where he gave them money for food.

He was sensitive and a troubled soul when he died.

When Alun visited us a year later, he brought his wife Bernadette with him and she and Mary enjoyed each other's company very much. They were living in Berlin and he'd just given up being conductor of an orchestra in Mexico but still owned the house in Troedyrhiw. When Gwyn had been diagnosed with throat cancer Alun insisted that he lived out his days with them in Berlin and on his death a huge bouquet in the shape of a piano was present at his funeral. A year later and using my new studio and thinking about my age I started to lean towards country music. Mary and me had always enjoyed what they called 'new country' which seemed to have more relevance both musically and lyrically. I suppose seeing the Everly Brothers at the Avan lido was something of an experience and now there were the Mavericks who we saw at the O2 Arena when they had their smash hit Dance the Night Away, and a few years later at St Davids Hall. I came up with a song The Last Train Out Of Sun Dance which Jeremy recorded and which appeared on a compilation by NBT Records of West Virginia in. Another song All The love We Need which I'd specifically written for Mary appeared on an album by Norwegian band Captain Kane and Big Trouble in two thousand and ten. This was due to the efforts of publisher and songwriter Peter Mason of Salisbury who was a friend and at one time had been in the band Dave Dee, Dozy, Mick and Titch. Unfortunately, over the years he developed Alzheimer's, and his publishing days had to end. It was not recorded as a duet as I'd written it but it had a good production and Iona and Andy have used it as a duet both here and in Ireland. Also, in that year a friend of mine sent me a DVD of a Thames Television children's program set in the nineteen sixties and what should be on it but my song Suburbia!

In the following year I met Hywel Jones and we 'hit it off' immediately. We chatted while his dog ran around the small park at the end of the road and I discovered that he'd suffered with cancer but that it was now in remission. He was also a Welsh speaker which gave me the opportunity to practice my Welsh and indeed his father had been something of a Welsh academic and had sent him and his sister to a Welsh school. Hywel was in his mid-fifties and had been a teacher until his cancer had occurred and the long treatment meant an end to his teaching profession. He was divorced but was on good terms with the two children from his first marriage who were in their twenties and who I met later at his house. He also had a son with his second wife Cathy, and we often met a Garth Olwg while I waited for Eli my grandson, and Hywel his son Elliot. We talked about music as Hywel had played drums in a band while living in Rhiwbina and I mentioned All The Love We Need which I'd dedicated to Mary and which had appeared on CD. He then asked if I would help him write a song which he could present to Cathy thanking her for the support she'd given him through his illness, and from then on, we spent many happy times in my studio over the next year or so where we composed a number of songs together.

Hywel always wanted to create the best demo recording possible and we often employed a studio in Nashville to do this for us and we were pleased with the results. After the four of us visited St Davids Hall to see a rock 'n roll review band Hywel seemed to be a little 'out of sorts' but I failed to see the significance until he mentioned that he was going back to see the cancer specialist.

During January of two-thousand and twelve Hywel received a reply from a friend of his Donna Lewis. She had fronted the band that he had played in and after he had sent her our song, Always It's You she said that she was happy to record it so that we could release it in aid of Tenovus a cancer charity for which he had been an ambassador. Donna who now lived in New York and had had hits both here and in America, enlisted the talents of among others Trevor Horne who produced it. Also, in January Hywel told me of Greg Lewis an independent producer/director who wanted to make a documentary about his battle with cancer filming him at various locations including at his home where I sat alongside him with my guitar and said something of our friendship. I wonder if it's a defect in my nature not to realise when someone is dying or maybe if I don't acknowledge it somehow, I can alter the inevitability of it all and that they will live. I felt the same about my brother. Hywel texted me while I was in a Welsh class to tell me that the cancer was back and that there was nothing they could do and the effect on me was overwhelming. How is it that the death of someone who I've only known for relatively short time could make such an impact? I visited him at his house and later at the hospice in Pontypridd until Cathy told me that it would be best if only she visited from then on. Hywell died on the 4th July two-thousand and twelve.

Greg was the first to state that when he started filming, he did not envisage such an ending. The programme went out on HTV with its title, Do Not Go Gentle. A Tribute To Hywel Jones. Prior to this we had been invited to take part in the Radio Wales show Good Morning Wales where the producer assured us that the record would be played regularly. It wasn't. The lady in charge of publicity for Tenovus while the real publicist was on maternity leave had no idea how to promote it. When I asked her if she would be visiting DJ's and pushing the record she replied "It's all done by e-mail now."!!! It has been used on a CD by the Tenovus Choir since and before 'lockdown' Donna has said that it will appear on her next album.

After Hywel's funeral I was distracted somewhat by a visit from Vaughan who had moved to Street in Somerset after his divorce from Lorna. She had arrived at the post office one day with grandson in her arms, to tell us that a new head master had taken over at Millfield and he was someone that Vaughan didn't get along with. Needless to say, that it wasn't in Vaughan's nature to compromise and when he was overlooked for a new position, he left without any thought of what he was going to do next and so he became a bus-driver. Fortunately, he then obtained a job working for a railway company at their offices at Ty Glas, Llanishen. I say fortunately, because his years spent in Somerset had left him with something of a west-country burr which some of the valley's people on his route took umbrage to even when he told them that he was Welsh and his father had actually been a freeman of Llantrisant!

# VALLEY LIGHTS

## Folk Songs of Wales Today

here is an album of songs in English by a variety of singers and
social attitudes in present day Wales, and some of these singers
king audiences — notably Frank Hennessy, Heather Jones, Mabsa

RITISH BOMB
GWNAETHPWYD
YNG NGHYMRU

ŴYL HEDDWCH
PEACE FESTIVAL
Music with Miwsig gan
DAFYDD IWAN · HEATHER
ROD THOMAS · KEVIN
ac eraill/and o
Cardiff
Hydre
tondina
od · Stalls

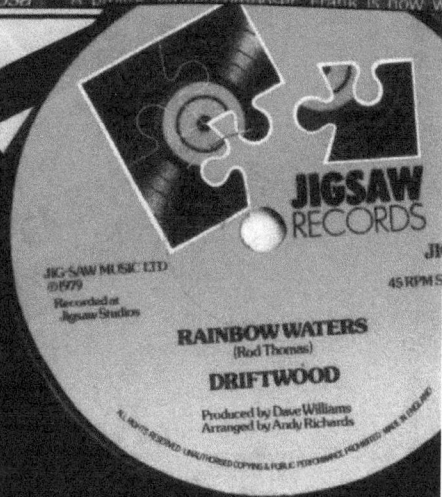

JIGSAW RECORDS

JIG-SAW MUSIC LTD
©1979
Recorded at
Jigsaw Studios

45 RPM

**RAINBOW WATERS**
(Rod Thomas)
**DRIFTWOOD**

Produced by Dave Williams
Arranged by Andy Richards

79

Hywel and me in my studio at Chandlers Reach, Llantwit Fardre.
Below right the song we wrote for the Tenovus Society, Always It's You.
To the left the cover of the compilation CD of Tim Andrews songs.
Below Mary and our stone at Pantmawr Cemetery, Rhiwbina.

They had bought a house in Brocastle and while living in the flat I agreed to do some electrical work there and all was well though things seemed a little strained. He could be selfish and when Lorna complained about having to cut the grass, he joked that he'd bought her 'a pucka motor-mower' that she could sit on! This was not a joke to Lorna however and things began to deteriorate and when we called in one day, we found Vaughan with a half-sized snooker table in the living room. Lorna had gone. She had said that if he bought that she would leave him. When I spoke to her a long time after this event, she said that she was sorry she hadn't left him years ago.

In fairness to Dewi who had taught with Vaughan at Pentyrch he hated the way Vaughan had treated Lorna and both he and Heulwen had found it hard to visit them. Signs I had obviously missed in their relationship.

Vaughan then had arrived on our doorstep to tell us that he was directing a pantomime at a village called Ashcott a few miles away from where he now lived, it was Treasure Island but he had no songs for it and asked if I could adapt some that I'd used in the children's musical and maybe write a few more? Welcoming the diversion, I obliged and recorded the songs they would use and backing tracks that would accompany them. Then at the end of October, two-thousand and twelve I receive an unexpected cheque from the secretary of the village hall committee and an invite to attend any of the performances in the November and December for which they were happy to cover bed and breakfast. Mary and me enjoyed our two days in the area visiting Street and Glastonbury where we also met Vaughan's girlfriend who was a member of the cast. She was a druidess and most interesting as many of their ideas complimented ours in humanism and humanitarianism. Alas this was something that Vaughan couldn't believe in and consequently they eventually separated. The show ran for three nights and was deemed a success and I appreciated the compliments that I received for my contribution.

In July of two-thousand and thirteen a collection of songs by Tim Andrews came out on a CD by RPM Records/Cherry Red who re-mastered the tracks so that the track and 'outtro' of Something About Suburbia was a good fifteen seconds longer than the original forty-five. It consisted of songs Tim had recorded with various bands before embarking on a solo career and the name of this new CD was Something About Suburbia/The Sixties Sounds of Tim Andrews. So, of all the tracks Tim recorded this was the one which due to air-play had stayed in people's minds May of two-thousand and thirteen was our fiftieth wedding anniversary. You'd had a stomach ulcer which we'd sorted out with a specialist and tablets. The ulcer had gone and we were ready to celebrate but as the year progressed the symptoms began to recur and the doctor suspected the ulcer had returned. In November you felt so ill that I took you to A & E but as we got there you started to groan and you were quickly admitted to surgery. It was sometime in the early hours that the surgeon came to me to tell me that things did not look good. He could operate but he didn't hold out much hope. Jeremy was with me and we asked him to do the best that he could. Sarah, Roger and Eli were travelling home from Manchester and were continually on the phone to Jeremy.

Mary died; the aneurism had been fatal. We said goodbye as tubes controlled the rise and fall of her chest. "Don't leave me!" I blurted out through my tears as the medical staff cast their eyes downwards. It was all so sudden.

"I was supposed to go first. Remember!" When we were young and Tom and Netta had spent the night with relatives and under the pretence of wall-papering I had stayed the night. My sock had a hole in it and I stuffed it in my shoe so that you wouldn't see it as we slipped into bed. And after, listening to the rain outside. Words of love. Hold me close tell me how you feel? Tell me love is real. And another night as a guest I slept in the box-room and you woke me with a Shh.... As you led me back to your room. God, I miss you. This has left me reeling. How am I supposed to go one without you? We shared everything; you were part of me. My life has ended.

Jeremy and Sarah were hurting, but rallied 'round. We cried as the three of us, arm in arm entered the crematorium to True Love Ways. Howard took the 'service' brilliantly as I knew he would even though it was something he'd never done before. The funeral director was sceptical until he had spoken to him, then he was won over completely. Being atheists, he wanted to know if he should cover the crosses but no, let those who believe, believe. And we sang a hymn. There is nothing like singing to bring people together.

Don Llewellyn could remember Mary as a child running up Temperance Road to watch the television with all the other kids at the house of Ernie Griffiths, one of the few televisions in the village at the time. Then Lyndon tried to say something but failed.

Alone in the house I cried, and then swore at you for not being here, then cried again. That was eight years ago, when my life changed never to be the same again. I'm a different person now but she's still with me every hour of every day.

Lyndon called with his dog, his son's dog actually on the first Saturday morning after Mary's funeral. "We're going up the Garth for a walk," he said, and we've done this almost every Saturday since. Bev brought ready-made meals to put in the micro-oven, and Howard and Dewi called in. His wife Heulwen was also a school teacher and had a lovely personality. From Llandovery she would always use cups and saucers when we called, and a milk-jug and sugar bowl, in the same way Netta had done and my aunties in Abercanaid. Her cancer had returned and in answer to our requests to visit he would say 'let her finish treatment first.' In truth he had given up school to look after her and within a few months she had also died. In the local pub at the beginning of December Sarah's friends tried to persuade me to accompany Sarah, Roger and Eli on a skiing holiday to Sol in Austria which had been arranged, and being carried along with their wishes we set off by car in a convoy with one overnight stop in Luxemburg. I stayed there for a week even taking skiing lessons with Sarah who never left my side, and then flew home from Innsbruck to spend Christmas with Jeremy.

In January of two-thousand and fourteen Ruth my niece put I Have Seen It All on YouTube. Using Dave Williams' production, I'd collected photographs and drawn others in readiness before losing Mary and Ruth graciously did the rest. Jeremy then suggested that we record two songs with the Cambrian Male Voice Choir. Fred Nicholas, the conductor had arranged the songs and Mary and me had gone up to Rhondda Heritage Park to hear them being performed. Dai Shell made himself instantly available to record them. He had called Mary 'his treasure' when she had taken him some apple tarts that she had made and it did seem that Dai and others wanted me to get involved, and keep me busy perhaps. Don asked me if I would return to the History Society which started back in the February and I did so. He told the members of my loss and thanked me for being there and I braced myself for the condolences at the end of the meeting.

And so, the year progressed still living at home but spending more time with Sarah and her family, a holiday in Spain with them and Luke, Roger's son by his first marriage and his grandson, Alfie. I began to go to Llantrisant Folk Club who met in Pontyclun and on a singer's night I would sing a song or two and later with Lyndon we performed a 'showcase' before going on to play in other folk clubs in Cardiff and Newport. Then in two-thousand and fifteen we recorded a CD of my songs at Long Row studios in Treforest and during this year also Timothy Jones was re-released on a compilation album of songs from the seventies under the title Mixed Up Minds 1969-1974.

Then when Lyndon and me played the village hall at Pentyrch the lady M C introduced me as being Lyndon's uncle. I looked at her questioningly and she said embarrassingly "Well he told me!" I think he likes the fact that we're related and I know he still misses Mary. We decided to sing more Everly Brothers songs and to this end we augmented our duo to become a rock 'n roll band using a drummer and Dai Shell as lead guitarist. This meant that I no longer had to worry about playing bits of lead guitar as I had done and I just strummed my guitar and sang. For a while we re hearsed in my old empty house, the music being a distraction.

When Mary was alive, we visited Howard often at his house in Rhiwbina. He'd finished working as a supply teacher at Glan Taf and was now a 'house husband' while Ann his second wife, taught English as a second language and children William and Elizabeth were at school. Since Mary's death I visited more often as his emphysema began to worsen and after he had had a few spells in hospital I made sure I was there when he needed me. He had met Ann when Claud his first wife had come back from Singapore to enable their two daughters Isabel and Catherine to go to school. Howard followed and prepped them as they walked to school to take their A-levels as they walked to school to take their A-levels after their divorce, he did the same thing with Elizabeth and William who attended Glan Taf but unfortunately, he didn't live to see Elizabeth's successful career in journalism when in July of two thousand and eighteen he died. When I spoke at his funeral, I found it hard to accept that Howard, my oldest friend had gone. He was the last link to my youth and yet another set of shared memories had died with him.

Lyndon and me still walked the Garth Mountain and debated as to whether we could see

Glastonbury Tor, or not and so in the summer of two-thousand and nineteen while Lyndon's wife and her sisters visited the Cavern Club, I booked a room for us in Glastonbury. It was also an opportunity to visit Vaughan who I hadn't seen since Mary's funeral and lived in nearby Street. We climbed the Tor and, in the evening, called in on Vaughan taking a bottle of whiskey with us to enjoy our night together. He now lived in sheltered accommodation after a few heart attacks and also the effects of diabetes. We were both shocked by his condition and his rather lonely existence but he appreciated our company and during the evening we suggested that he might think about moving back to south Wales.

The following morning, we called again intending to take him for a coffee before we left but he declined saying he was expecting a 'home help to call. In January of two-thousand and twenty his daughter Anna phoned to say that he had died and that I was executor of his will, he had also asked her to look for similar accommodation back home in south Wales, but it wasn't to be.

Vaughan could be stubborn, petulant and even selfish but I liked him.

Now I'm sitting on the decking at the front of the house looking down over Baglan and Swansea Bay and wondering if there's anything left in store me.

Timothy Jones has been re-released on yet another compilation CD called Bub bler- Rock Is Here to Stay but I don't envisage any more of my songs being used as the music scene has changed so much, vinyl to CD and now the ether via the 'web'.

Jeremy is a few miles away at Bryn in the house Mary secured for him in nineteen eighty-nine. His son Jacob was the result of a relationship which didn't work out. His then partner Ellie, turned out to be by-polar but unfortunately vindictive when we had spent time making a home for them to live. Thankfully after some troubled years over visiting rights, Jake now spends most of his time with Jeremy. He continues to play in the Hightider's band who accompany tribute artists particularly during the Elvis Festival at Porthcawl and we still write together.

Sarah is working in her 'new' house while Roger is working from home in his study and Eli is at Swansea University. I sometimes feel like an appendage, an add-on but hopefully not a burden.

In nineteen seventy-eight a year after Mum had died, we took Dad down to Meidrim to explore his and my roots and met Benjie an ex-postman who was the same age as Dad and who had also lost his wife. He was very friendly and helpful and he took some photographs D'cu had brought up from Meidrim in the hope that someone might recognise them and perhaps name some of them, but alas the passage of time had been too great. His mother however, had worked for Jenkin Thomas of the Fountain Inn who had married Dad's great Aunt and later Benjie sent us a photo of him.

In nineteen-eighty-seven we visited Meidrim again on our way to Pembroke and we discovered Benjie sitting in the sun in his front garden sound asleep. "You're not going to wake him?" Mary asked. No. Let him sleep and dream of his father and mother, his wife, his children and his friends and all the events that had happened in his life.

All THE LOVE WE NEED
Rod Thomas

IF YOU'RE FEELING LOW ON A RAINY DAY,

I'LL GIVE YOU COMFORT ALONG THE WAY,

WE'LL PLAN OUR LIFE AND SET OUR COURSE

AND RIDE OUT OUR TROUBLES ON THIS TRUSTY HORSE,


AND OUR LOVE WON'T LET US DOWN, EVEN ON THE STONY GROUND,

IN OUR HEARTS WE'RE AS SURE AS WE CAN BE,

AND NO MATTER WHERE WE GO, THIS LOVE WILL ALWAYS FLOW,

LIKE A RIVER CARRYING YOU AND ME,

WE HAVE ALL THE LOVE WE NEED,


IN TIMES OF DOUBT WHERE THE ROADS DIVIDE,

I'LL LIFT YOUR SPIRITS I'LL BE YOUR GUIDE,

IF THE WAY IS DARK, WE'LL HOLD ON TIGHT,

AND RIDE THROUGH TOGETHER INTO THE LIGHT,


WE'LL NEVER LOOK BACK JUST KEEP TRAVELLING ON,

WE'LL STICK TO THE TRACK TWO LIVING AS ONE,


AND OUR LOVE WON'T LET US DOWN, EVEN ON THE STONY GROUND,

IN OUR HEARTS WE'RE AS SURE AS WE CAN BE,

AND NO MATTER WHERE WE GO, THIS LOVE WILL ALWAYS FLOW

LIKE A RIVER CARRYING YOU AND ME,

WE HAVE ALL THE LOVE WE NEED,

WE HAVE ALL THE LOVE WE NEED.

**TIM ANDREWS:** "(Something About) Suburbia" (Parlophone)

Ah, that a bit better. I don't know who it is. Where the hell's suburbia? I like the beat. I love that vaudeville drum bit. It's nice to dance to—catchy. I don't think it is going to crash into the charts but it's going to be played. It's sweet. I love a record with a strong beat. Lousy record player.

---

Tim ("Sad Simon Lives Again") Andrews is moving from his Bayswater, London, home because he claims his flat is haunted. His new single "Something About Suburbia" is out tomorrow (Friday). Maybe that's where he should move to!

---

## TIM ANDREWS

**SUBURBIA** (Parlophone)—For all all those destroyed by the mere sight of hundreds of semis surrounded by a few mangy trees, five o'clock tea and orange juice at the clinic this is not for you. Mr. Andrews, who is very sweet and vocally reminds me of Mr. Marriott in a way, actually WANTS to go back to it all. He's fed up with swinging London—and who can blame him?

TIM ANDREWS does a very good job on "(Something About) Suburbia" (Parlophone R 5695), in a clickety-click sort of sing-along item on an unusual topic. Good sense of style might be a hit.

**OUT TOMORROW**

---

## TIM ANDREWS

---

# Song in the air for pop writer Rod

**Mr. Roderick Thomas**

THERE'S a song in the air for 23-year-old electrician Roderick Thomas these days and its "Something About Suburbia."

That's the title of a pop song that Roderick wrote that's getting plenty of air time lately.

Roderick is the son of Mr. and Mrs. Eddie Thomas, now of Rhiwbina, Cardiff, but formerly of Troedyrhiw and Abercanaid respectively.

Rod's aunt, Mrs. Emlyn Francis, of Glantaff Stores, Troedyrhiw, (herself the mother of a talented pair of musicians, Alun and Gwyn Francis) confirmed that the number is getting plenty of time on Radio Luxembourg and the BBC pop shows.

the help and encouragement of his guitar playing accountant brother Malcolm. Then they tape record the result.

Married with two children, Jeremy aged four and Sarah aged one, Rod now lives at Pentyrch, near Cardiff.

In true romantic 'moon and June' tradition he married his childhood sweetheart, Mary.

And that's obviously a theme for a song.

---

**TIM ANDREWS:** "Something About Suburbia" (Parlophone). It's a bird singing a bit like Stevie Marriott.

Hang about, my mate the unemployed portrait painter has just informed me: "It's a bloke." Oh well, of course it could be a ferret. Who knows in these troubled times.

Heavy four to the bar, brass. Catchy tune, fairly interesting lyrics.

---

Friday, May 3, 1968

# Composer Cuts New Disc

*Mr. Roderick Thomas pictured here with his wife and two young children.*

WINNERS of the Song for Wales contest run by the BBC Wales TV folk programme *Gwerin 74* are Anglesey lyricist Robin Griffith (right) and Rod Thomas, of Pentyrch, South Wales, who composed the music. Their song —the English title is *To Make Wales Free*—will be the Welsh entry in the Pan-Celtic Festival Song Competition in Killarney this weekend. Rod and Robin, who have been writing songs together for two years, apart from the £50 first prize, took a £25 second prize for their other entry. Last year their songs took third and fourth places.

PENTYRCH musician Rod Thomas and his North Wales friend Robin Griffith swept the board in the BBC Wales Song For Wales contest on Saturday.

Twenty - eight - year - old Rod (pictured above), the composer, and Robin, the lyricist, won both the top prizes in the contest which was run in the Gwerin 74 television series.

First was their song Cael Cymru's Rydd (To Make Wales Free) and second their Fy Nghydwybod i (My Conscience). They received a £50 prize as winners and as runners-up, a £25 one. The prizes were presented by Mr. Owen Edwards, the Head of Programmes.

### Festival

Iris Williams, the Tonyrefail-born artiste, sang the songs in the contest and the best, selected from an original entry of 60, will now represent Wales in the Pan-Celtic Festival being held in Killarney on Saturday.

Rod and Robin have been writing songs together for two years—and in the same contest last year two of their creations came third and fourth.

## Their songs win top prizes

PENTYRCH singer and songwriter Rod Thomas and North Walian partner Robin Griffith won the top prizes in the B.B.C. Wales song contest "Song for Wales" on Saturday.

Rod wrote the music and Robin the lyrics for the winning song "Cael Cymru yn Gymru'n rydd" (Make Wales Free) and second placed "Fy Nghydwybod I" (My Conscience). Mr. Owen Edwards, Head of Programmes B.B.C. Wales, presented the £50 first prize and £25 second to the successful pair at the end of the Welsh language pop programme "Gwerin 74".

Rod, who lives with wife Mary and children Jeremy and Sarah at 19, Heol Dan-yr-Odyn has written songs for many artists, including Lulu.

His latest venture is an E.P. record, featuring him as part of a duo, accompanied by Lyndon Jones.

Rod and Robin's songs were sung on the programme by Tonyrefail born Iris Williams. "Make Wales Free" now goes on to represent Wales in Saturday's Pan-Celtic Festival at Killarney, Eire.

## IRIS SINGS IN KILLARNEY

SINGER Iris Williams represents Wleas in the Pan Celtic Festival in Killarney tomorrow.

She will be singing Cael Cyru's Rydd (To Make Wales Free) by Rod Thomas, of Pentyrch, and Robin Griffith, of North Wales, which won the Song for Wales contest last week.

# Yr ŵyl Ryng Geltaidd yn Cilairne

Ni allwn lai na meddwl am Bendigeidfran yn croesi o Harlech i Iwerddon gynt i ddelio a Matholwch, wrth i griw ohonom o Gymru a Chernyw groesi o Abertawe i Corc. Dim ond dychymyg breuddwydiol oedd hynny, roedd yr achos yn un llawer hapusach y tro hwn. Roeddem i gyd ar y ffordd i'r Wyl Ryng-Geltaidd yn Cilairne neu Killarney i ymuno a'r gweddill o'r cenhedloedd Celtaidd.

Croeso dibendraw gan y Gwyddelod, pobl yn aros ar y stryd i gael sgwrs. Nid myth yw'r hanesyn am gusannu carreg y Blarney - mae gan y Gwyddelod ffraethineb godidog. Un o'r hogia sy'n gyrru cart a cheffyl, jarvis yw'r enw arnynt, yn troi ataf a dweud mewn acen Wyddelig - "Facw mae stad Killarney. Miliwner sy bia'r

lle. Un ferch sydd ganddo ac fe drodd hi'n lliian. Dyna pam dydw i ddim wedi mynd i'r drafferth i'w nabod o".

Daeth uchafbwynt yr wythnos i ni pan ddaeth dyfarniad y beirniaid ar y gystadleuaeth Ryng-Geltaidd. Roeddem ni eisoes wedi cynnal cystadleuaeth ar GWERIN 74, a chân Rod Thomas a Robin Griffith "Cael Cymru yn Gymru Rydd" yn ennill. Roedd hi'n hwre fawr arnom ni'r Cymry pan ddyfarnwyd y gân yn gydradd gyntaf gyda chan hyfryd o Iwerddon. Iris Williams oedd yn ei chanu, a'r Diliau gyda hi. Pawb ohonom yno am anfon adref i ddweud, drwy'r teleffon y tro hwn, nid anfon y drudwy.

Rhydderch Jones

Iris Williams

# IRIS WILLIAMS

*yn canu caneuon buddugol Cystadleuaeth "Gwerin 74"*

Ochr 1

1. 'I Gael Cymru'n Gymru Rydd'
(Alaw Rod Thomas : Geiriau Robin Gruffydd)

2. 'Dyma Fi'
(Alaw Pete Griffiths : Geiriau Siân Edwards)

Ochr 2

1. 'Fy Nghydwybod'
(Alaw Rod Thomas : Geiriau Robin Gruffydd)

2. 'Angel'
(Geiriau ac Alaw Tecwyn Ifan)

Ar y record hon, clywir Iris Williams yn canu'r bedair cân a ddyfarnwyd yn orau yng nghystadleuaeth "Gwerin 74" BBC Cymru. Pedair cân sy'n adlewyrchu'r sefyllfa gyfoes ym myd caneuon gwreiddiol Cymraeg, a phedair cân sy'n amrywio'n fawr o ran naws ac arddull. Un peth sy'n nodweddiadol o'r canu cyfoes yng Nghymru yw fod y cyfansoddwyr hyn i gyd yn berfformwyr hefyd. I gyflwyno'r caneuon, llais cynnes-gyfoethog y ferch o Donyrefail—Iris Williams.

\*

Iris Williams sings on this record the four winning songs from the 1974 BBC Wales songwriting competition. These songs reflect some of the best qualities in the current Welsh pop scene, and it is noteworthy that the three composers represented here are also performers in their own right—Rod Thomas from the duo Rod a Lyndon, Pete Griffiths who is Eleri Llwyd's versatile accompanist, and Tecwyn Ifan from the widely acclaimed group 'Ac Eraill'.

Recordiad y BBC ; Cyfarwyddwr Cerdd Benny Litchfield
Atgynhyrchwyd trwy ganiatâd y BBC

*Cynlluniwyd y clawr gan Wyn ap Gwilym*

## A record from Iris

BBC Wales should further establish itself as a prime stimulator of the Welsh pop music scene as a result of a new E.P. record.

On the disc, I Gael Cymru'n Gymru Rydd, Tonyrefail-born Iris Williams sings the four winning songs from this year's songwriting competition, run via the Saturday television show Gwerin '74. The main song (To Make Wales Free) took Iris to success when she won the Pan Celtic Song Festival at Killarney in May — with credit owing, too, of course, to composer Rod Thomas, of Pentyrch.

The composers of all four songs on the record (Sain 46E) are frequently heard on BBC Wales programmes, so they plainly owe the Beeb—or should I coin the word Lleeb? — quite a bit. They are Rod, Pete Griffiths, who is Eleri Llwyd's accompanist, and Tecwyn Ifan, from the group Ac Eraill.

## ROD THOMAS

On his recent national talent-spotting tour, Jonathan King "discovered" and signed a Pentyrch electrician called Rod Thomas.

King, Britain's top singles producer, signed only two of the hopeful artists who sent him 600 demo records and tapes.

Rod sent him a tape of Timothy Jones, a song he wrote himself. He made the demonstration disc at Rockfield, near Monmouth, double-tracking his voice and playing piano and mellotron. Dave Edmunds, who happened to be in the studio at the time, overdubbed the drums.

When King heard the tape he asked Rod to go to London to record the song. Rod found him "very professional" to work with.

"He sets a fantastic pace," said Rod. "The day we made Timothy Jones, he recorded three other A-sides, including Flirt. And his singles don't often miss."

Rod's song has a strong lyric, about a young boy who seems more self-reliant than he really is. The backing is a big brassy sound, with strings on the chorus.

He has been signed by Fly Records and 'Timothy Jones' will be the first single to be released on their newly formed Cube label, a label being launched by the Essex Music Group, and will be released on May 19th.

He has written a number of songs and had a couple used by other artists. In 1968 his Something About Suburbia was recorded by Tim Andrews, and got a lot of airplays.

Rod, aged 27, is married with two children, and lives at Heol Dan-yr-Odin, Pentyrch, near Cardiff. Timothy Jones is not his first venture into show business.

DAVID RUFFELL (Press Officer)
May 1972

## CUBE RECORDS

on House, 68 Oxford Street, London \

Ochr 1
* JOSEFF
PAID Â PHOENI

Ochr 2
CERI
CANA GÂN

Mae Rod a Lyndon wedi bod yn canu gyda'i gilydd
am bum mlynedd. Daw Rod, sy'n chware'r gitâr ac
yn 'sgrifennu'r caneuon, o Bentyrch, Sir
Forgannwg, a daw Lyndon o Rydyfelin. Ef sy'n
chware'r gitâr bas.

Maent wedi ymddangos yn rheolaidd ar Disc a
Dawn. 'Roedd dwy o'r caneuon ar y record hon,
"Ceri" a "Cana Gân" ymysg y chwech gorau a
ddewiswyd ar gyfer cystadleuaeth Cân Disc a
Dawn y llynedd. Sonia'r gân "Joseph", am fywyd
cynnar y cyfansoddwr Dr. Joseph Parry.

* Recordiwyd y gân hon yn
Stiwdios y Ddraig, Caerdydd.
Cefndir lleisiol gan "Y Diliau."

ROD THOMAS

Rod Thomas — "Timothy Jones." Of the Cube releases, I feel this Jonathan King production is the "commercial" one of the trio. Basically a look into the misunderstanding and lack of liaison that parents have with their offsprings, this is an interesting composition by Rod Thomas, which he handles in a professional manner.
(Cube Bug 19).

**ROD THOMAS 'Timothy Jones' (Cube).** Fly records have changed their name to Cube. Following Jonathan King's recent talent scouting venture, he wound up accepting two artists out of the 600 applications. Rod Thomas is one of them and Jonathan has produced and directed his debut. The song is a commercial effort about a man who isn't quite all he seems to be.

JONATHAN KING is launching new singer Rod Thomas, whom he discovered during his nationwide talent search. Rod's debut single "Timothy Jones" will be the first release on the Essex Music Group's new Cube label in about six weeks.

# Rod gets a break

## By Ken Follett

ON his recent national talent-spotting tour, Jonathan King "discovered" and signed a Pentyrch electrician called Rod Thomas.

King, Britain's top singles producer, signed only two of the hopeful artists who sent him 600 demo records and tapes.

Rod sent him a tape of Timothy Jones, a song he wrote himself. He made the demonstration disc at Rockfield, near Monmouth, double - tracking his voice and playing piano and mellotron. Dave Edmunds, who happened to be in the studio at the time, overdubbed the drums.

When King heard the tape he asked Rod to go to London to re-record the song. Rod found him "very professional" to work with.

"He sets a fantastic pace," said Rod. "The day we made Timothy Jones, he recorded three other A-sides, including Flirt. And his singles don't often miss."

Rod's song has a strong lyric, about a young boy who seems more self-reliant than he really is. The backing is a big brassy sound, with strings on the chorus.

It has been bought by Cube, a new label being launched by the Essex Music Group, and will be released in about six weeks.

Rod, aged 27, is married with two children, and lives at Heol Dan-yr-Odin, Pentyrch, near Cardiff. Timothy Jones is not his first venture into show business.

He has written a number of songs, and had a couple used by other artists. In 1968 his Something About Suburbia was recorded by Tim Andrews, and got a lot of airplays.

He is due to appear on HTV Wales's Cantamil on Monday at 4.15 p.m., singing with friend Lyndon Jones, of Rhydyfelin, Pontypridd, a Welsh translation of one of his songs, Peter Pan.

Essex Music introduced their new Cube label, which will eventually replace the highly successful Fly logo, with a superb presentation at one of London's oldest theatres, the Criterion, in Piccadilly Circus. From the initial signings, folk singer Harvey Andrews emerges the most impressive with his highly imaginative songs which he superbly interpreted with a simple guitar accompaniment. The presentation opened with soul man Jimmy Helms who proved to be a more than competent performer, while jazz rock unit the Gasoline Band, who closed the show, was somewhat disappointing. Fourth Cube signing, Rod Thomas did not appear due to prior commitments, although he should make some impact with his first single "Timothy Jones." Harvey Andrews, however, has the necessary qualities for long-term success and gives Cube a fine start with a single, "In The Darkness" and album, "Writer Of Songs."

## King Cube
## ROD THOMAS

A new artist discovered by the ubiquitous Jonathan King during his nationwide talent search at the end of last year. ROD THOMAS here performs his own composition – produced and directed by JK. It's a single called TIMOTHY JONES BUG 19. And it'll be another King-size hit for the country's leading singles producer (Music Week 1971 chart analysis).

| Y Gân | Cyfansoddwr | Perfformwyr | |
|---|---|---|---|
| Cydio'n Dynn | Llion Jones, Euros Jones | Eryr Wen | ☐ |
| I'r Wyres Fach | Nia Griffith, Gwenda Williams, Glyn Roberts | Nia a Gwenda | ☐ |
| Ar ôl y Gwin | Emlyn Dole | Y Brodyr Gregory | ☐ |
| Lliwiau | Heulwen Evans, Gwenno Dafydd | Heulwen a Gwenno | ☐ |
| Y Rasta Gwyn | Bryn Fôn, Rhys Parry | Sobin a'r Smaeliaid | ☐ |
| Cyn i'r Dieithriad Ddod | Rod Thomas, Robin Griffith | Bedwyr Morgan | ☐ |
| Gwylio'r Cymylau | Enfys Tanner, Eluned Rees | Catrin Mair | ☐ |
| Dagrau'r De | Maldwyn Pope, Gareth Morlais | Maldwyn a Gareth | ☐ |

Am y tro cyntaf erioed yn ei hanes derbyniwyd nawdd i gystadleuaeth *Cân i Gymru* eleni sy'n golygu y bydd y cyfansoddwr/cyfansoddwyr buddugol yn derbyn gwobr o £1,000, yn ogystal â thlws gwydr hardd.

Derbyniwyd y nawdd gan y gymdeithas gydweithredol, Co-operative Retail Services, sydd â nifer o siopau ar hyd a lled Cymru. Yn ôl Huw Jones o Deledu'r Tir Glas, y cwmni teledu annibynnol sy'n gyfrifol am drefnu'r gystadleuaeth, a'r telediad, roedd penderfyniad cwmni CRS i noddi'r gystadleuaeth yn 'adlewyrchu'r ffaith fod hon yn gystadleuaeth bwysig yng

**CARDIFF INDEPENDENT™ "CHILDREN OF THE OAK"**

BARE feet may not suit March's temperatures but Llanedeyrn High School pupils are a hardy lot. They are seen here following a final costume fitting for Children of the Oak before the performances today (Thursday) and tom (7.3

**Childrens Choir**
Funiculi Funicula
Pie Jesu
Travel the Road
At the End of the Day

**TONYREFAIL CHILDREN'S CHOIR**
Travel The Road . . . . . . . . . . . . . . . .
Y Mae Afon . . . . . . . . . . . . . . . . . . . .
Thanks Be To God . . . . . . . . . . . . . . .

**3. Tonyrefail Children's Choir**
a) Travel the Road

# 'NIBLO' WAS THE BEST
## ... and that's from the conductor of the Berlin Philharmonic

L. Denza
A. Lloyd Webber
Rod Thomas

ONE of Merthyr's greatest musicians and characters - honky-tonk dustman Gwyn 'Niblo' Francis who has died at the age of 51 - was paid the highest tribute yesterday.

For his twin brother Alun - principal conductor of the Berlin Philharmonic Orchestra - admitted: "Gwyn was the better musician."

The brothers grew up in Troedyrhiw and received identical musical training. Gwyn became a rock 'n' roll pianist and Alun an internationally renowned composer and conductor.

"He was much more naturally gifted than me but he had no patience at all," said Alun from Milan where he is in concert tonight.

"I have conducted more than 100 orchestras but the one with the talent was the man at the pub piano in Troedyrhiw.

"We were both given piano lessons as children. But we soon discovered that for the price of two lessons we could have five games of snooker at Sam Bezani's coffee shop in Bridge Street - the Las Vegas of Troedyrhiw.

"We gave up piano lessons and by the age of 15 we'd formed a pop group called the Bow Ties - we'd do all the Everly Brothers' songs."

Meanwhile Alun stuck to his studies and won a place at the Royal Manchester College of Music while Gwyn went on to form his own rock 'n' roll group, Niblo's People, supporting top artistes such as Matt

**EXCLUSIVE**
BY TONY TRAINOR

Gwyn would strip down a piano, removing the top and front panels, and hammer out Little Richard songs to the amazement of his friends.

He once wheeled a piano to Troedyrhiw Square and gave an impromptu open air concert on Christmas Day. Gwyn later became a warehouse manager at Tesco in Merthyr, before becoming a road sweeper and dustman for Merthyr Borough Council.

"Over the years I dedicated a few pieces of music to Gwyn," said Alun. "When I knew he was going to die I wanted to send a piece to him as soon as possible.

"I said, 'What do you think?'

"He replied: 'I'm reserving judgement'."

A fortnight before his death Gwyn was proud to hear that the latest piece from Alun, *Intrada*, was publically dedicated to him before an audience of more than 20,000 people at the Verona Open Air Festival.

At his funeral service Gwyn's recreations were listed as the Belle Vue, the Ex Club and the Green Meadow.

"My brother was fond of a drink and anything could happen after it," said Alun.

"He once told the manager of the BBC Orchestra that they weren't very good. And he complained that at the Albert Hall you

**'The one with the talent was the man at the pub piano in Troedyrhiw.'**
– Alun Francis

**MUSICAL ENIGMA:** The late Gwyn "Niblo" Francis, a better musician than twin brother Alun, conductor of the Berlin Philharmonic Orchestra?

ARTHUR HOWES, ACUFF ROSE & E MANAGEMENT present

THE WORLD'S No. 1 HIT RECORDER
**ROY ORBISON**

THE EXCITING! FABULOUS!
**WALKER BROTHERS**

LITTLE MISS DYNAMITE **LULU**

PARLOPHONE RECORDING ARTISTES
**THE MARIONETTES**

**KIM D AND THE DEL 5**

YOUR COMPERE RAY CAMERON — NOW BOOKING

**THE QUOTATIONS**

**MARCH**
FINSBURY PARK, Astoria — Fri 25th, 7.10 & 9.10
BIRMINGHAM, Odeon — Sat 26th, 6.00 & 8.30
WALTHAMSTOW, Granada — Mon 28th, 6.30 & 8.10
CHESTER, A.B.C. — Tues 29th, 6.15 & 8.30
WIGAN, A.B.C. — Wed 30th, 6.30 & 8.35
GLASGOW, Odeon — Thur 31st, 6.40 & 9.00

**APRIL**
EDINBURGH, A.B.C. — Fri 1st, 6.30 & 8.50
NEWCASTLE, City Hall — Sat 2nd, 6.15 & 8.45
LEEDS, Odeon — Sun 3rd, 5.30 & 8.00
WOLVERHAMPTON, Gaumont — Tues 5th, 6.30 & 8.40
MANCHESTER, Odeon — Wed 6th, 6.15 & 8.45
STOCKTON, A.B.C. — Thur 7th, 6.15 & 8.30
BRADFORD, Gaumont — Fri 8th, 6.15 & 8.40
EAST HAM, Granada — Sat 9th, 6.30 & 8.00

**APRIL**
LEICESTER, De Montfort Hall — Sun 10th, 5.40 & 8.00
BLACKPOOL, Odeon — Mon 11th, 6.00 & 8.30
BRISTOL, Colston Hall — Thur 14th, ... & 8.45
CARDIFF, Capitol — Fri 15th, 6.15 & 8.50
SHEFFIELD, City Hall — Sat 16th, 6.10 & 8.40
LIVERPOOL, Empire — Sun 17th, 5.40 & 8.00
OXFORD, New Theatre — Wed 20th, 6.15 & 8.30
DUBLIN, Adelphi — Thur 21st, 6.30 & 8.00
BELFAST, A.B.C. — Fri 22nd, 6.45 & 9.00
HAMMERSMITH, Odeon — Sat 23rd, 6.45 & 9.00
IPSWICH, Gaumont — Sun 24th, 5.30 & 8.00
TOOTING, Granada — Wed 27th, 7.00 & 9.10
LUTON, Ritz — Thur 28th, 6.30 & 8.45
PORTSMOUTH, Guildhall — Fri 29th, 6.30 & 8.50
BOURNEMOUTH, Winter Gdns. — Sat 30th, 6.00 & 8.15

**MAY**
COVENTRY, Coventry Theatre — Sun 1st, 6.00 & 8.30

Kim 'D' AND THE Del 5

**DRIFTWOOD:** 'Rainbow Waters' (Jigsaw Jig 1)

If there is such a thing as Pastoral Rock, Driftwood might well be leading the field. . .ha-ha — well, please yourself.

'Rainbow Waters' is a formal, Scottish-type lilt which smacks of lochs and heathered downs, with most of the melody being taken by a doubled synth and guitar line. There are plenty of ear-tickling bagpipish keyboards in the background which flesh out the sound and push the tune to the front.

Somehow there's the impression that it ought to be sung by a classroom full of kids. There's an almost hymn-book completeness to the melody which comes round in a neat circle over some solid, paced, if a little ponderous drumming.

The centre break is a brief guitar solo made by majestic string-synth chords underneath and a great synth brass section, very close to trumpets.

An instrumental, and as such destined to be talked over by DJ's or used as backing material for some public information film about a ruined castle. Worth more if only because Driftwood are in fact four musicians better known as The Strawbs.

JIGSAW RECORDS LAUNCH

Dave Williams' Jigsaw operation branches out into the record industry with its own label on 2nd November, 1979. Jigsaw Records makes its debut with a distinctive instrumental single - "RAINBOW WATERS" by DRIFTWOOD, produced by Dave Williams.

Driftwood are comprised of Brian Willoughby (guitar), Andy Richards (keyboards), Chas Cronk (bass) and Tony Fernandez (drums) and are better known for their work under the banner of The Strawbs.

Williams has always been an enthusiastic innovator of original ideas but has concentrated, in the past, mainly on the development of new talent.  As producer, he launched the careers of CAMEL, PHIL CORDELL (alias SPRINGWATER) and GARY BENSON before working with the legendary IKE & TINA TURNER. In the mid-seventies he diverted his efforts towards building Jigsaw Studios and also developed an impressive music publishing catalogue.

Now, with the studio established and the publishing company being administered by Ron McCreight's RMO Music, Williams once again is concentrating on production, with Jigsaw Records providing an ideal outlet.

Several other single and album projects are now underway, but right now, the haunting Rod Thomas melody, "Rainbow Waters" gives the label a dignified beginning.

## Behind the Scenes

Vaughan Williams

| | |
|---|---|
| Director | Vaughan Williams |
| Composer | Rod Thomas |
| Stage Manager | Jane Morton |
| Assistant Stage Manager | Paul Stevens |
| Scenery & Props | SPLATLOT: Guinnie Amesbury, Nina Amesbury, Nicky Brooks, Ellis Evans, Imogen LeHunte, Jonathan Lehunte, Matthew LeHunte, Jane Morton, Joe Parkman, Jane Speakman, Betty Spearing, Miles Stevens, Paul Stevens |
| Back Stage Crew | Tom Buck, Ellis Evans, Dave LeHunte, Imogen LeHunte, Jonathan LeHunte, Ian Morton, Joe Parkman, Reuben Whitcombe |
| Lighting | David Adkins, Guy Hunt-Davison |
| Sound | Tom Davies, Andy Harvey |
| Sound Apprentice | Sam Hughes |
| Prompt | Nicki Hunt-Davison |
| Make-up | Veronica Acreman, Celia Cromey Hawke, Elaine Hayne, Nicki Hunt-Davison, Sue Knight |
| Wardrobe | Anita Clarke, Jackie Hawkins |
| Fight Scene | Arranged by Nicki Hunt-Davison |
| Production Team | Lyn Harvey, Nicki Hunt-Davison, Jane Morton, Sue Wilton |
| Programme | John Herbert |

On behalf of the Village Hall Management Committee, I would like to say a very big thank you to all the people that make our Pantomime the great success that it always is. It is impossible to mention everybody by name but we really do appreciate all the 'back room' boys and girls, mothers and fathers and all those who do so much to make it run smoothly. I must mention the cast themselves and the parents and friends of the younger members who do so much chauffering to get the children to the numerous rehearsals.

Also, I would like to thank Ashcott Stores (Londis) and The Ring O' Bells for selling the tickets beforehand on our behalf.

*Jenny Todman, Chairman*

## ASHCOTT PANTO 2012

presents

# Treasure Island

Based on an original script by Ian Ritchie
Adapted by Vaughan Williams & Pat Mead

Music by Rod Thomas
Directed by Vaughan Williams

## ASHCOTT VILLAGE HALL

Thursday 29th November,
Friday 30th November,
Saturday 1st December
7.30 p.m.

**Saturday Matinee**
1st December
2.30 p.m.

**PROGRAMME 20p**

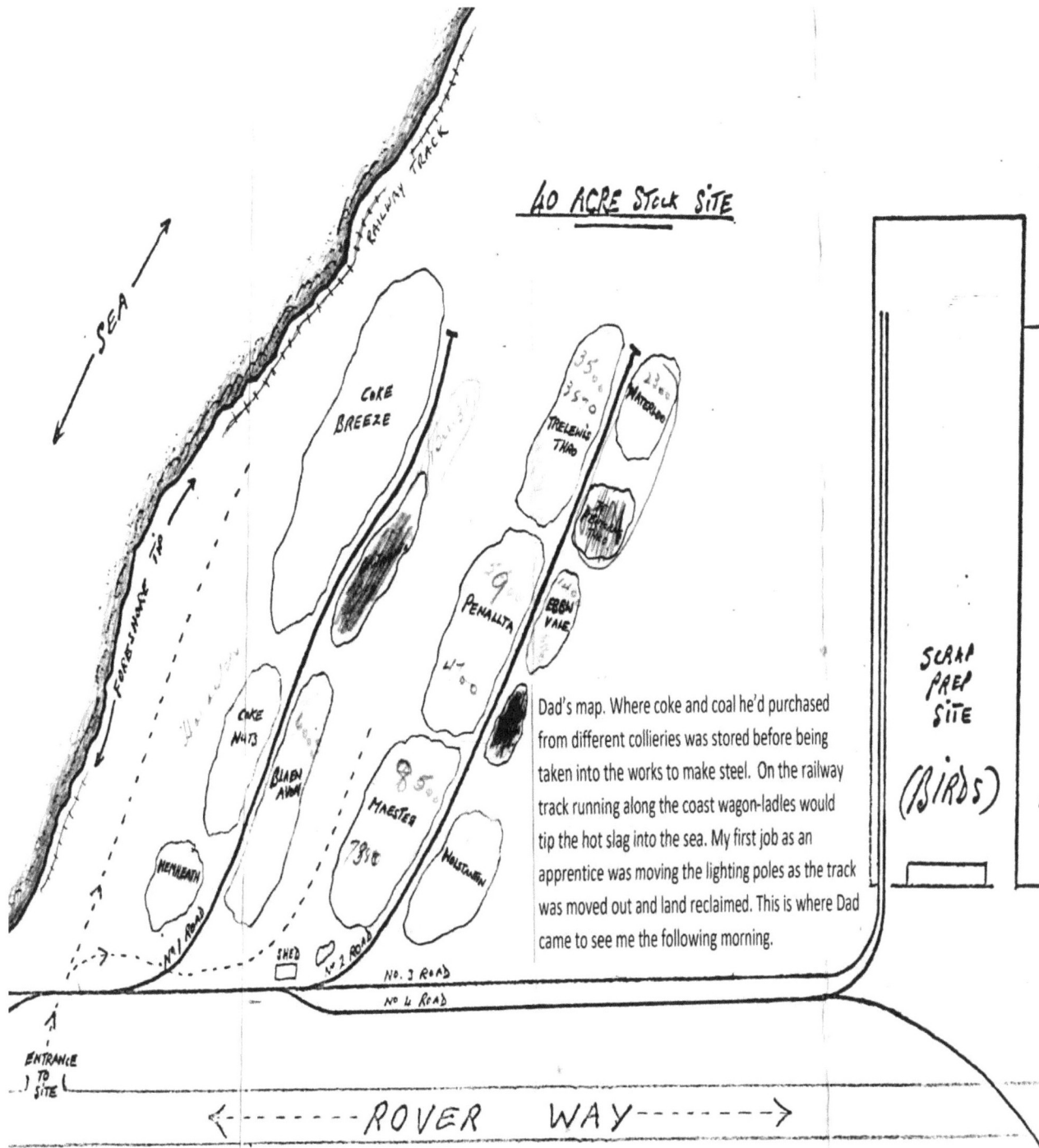

40 ACRE STOCK SITE

SEA

RAILWAY TRACK

FORESHORE TIP

COKE BREEZE

TRELEWIS THRO

WATERLOO

PENALLTA

9 PENALLTA

EBBW VALE

COKE NUTS

BLAEN AVON

MAESTEG

HENLLEATH

NANTGARW

SHED

NO.1 ROAD

NO.2 ROAD

NO. 3 ROAD

NO. 4 ROAD

ENTRANCE TO SITE

SCRAP PREP SITE

(BIRDS)

Dad's map. Where coke and coal he'd purchased from different collieries was stored before being taken into the works to make steel. On the railway track running along the coast wagon-ladles would tip the hot slag into the sea. My first job as an apprentice was moving the lighting poles as the track was moved out and land reclaimed. This is where Dad came to see me the following morning.

ROVER WAY

Milton Keynes UK
Ingram Content Group UK Ltd.
UKHW051841290324
440070UK00002B/3

9 781963 789072